SOMEWHERE OUT THERE

When Norma Jean Clarke-McCloud, BA(Hons), was told in 1986, at forty years of age, that she was the child of a World War II, G.I. soldier, her world was turned upside down, and she vowed she would not rest until she had tracked him down.

Seven gruelling, often frustrating years later, with the spectre of rejection ever foremost in her mind, she finally reaches her goal and comes face to face with the father whose image had fuelled her driving ambition.

What happens next will bring a tear to the hardest heart and hope to all those following in her footsteps.

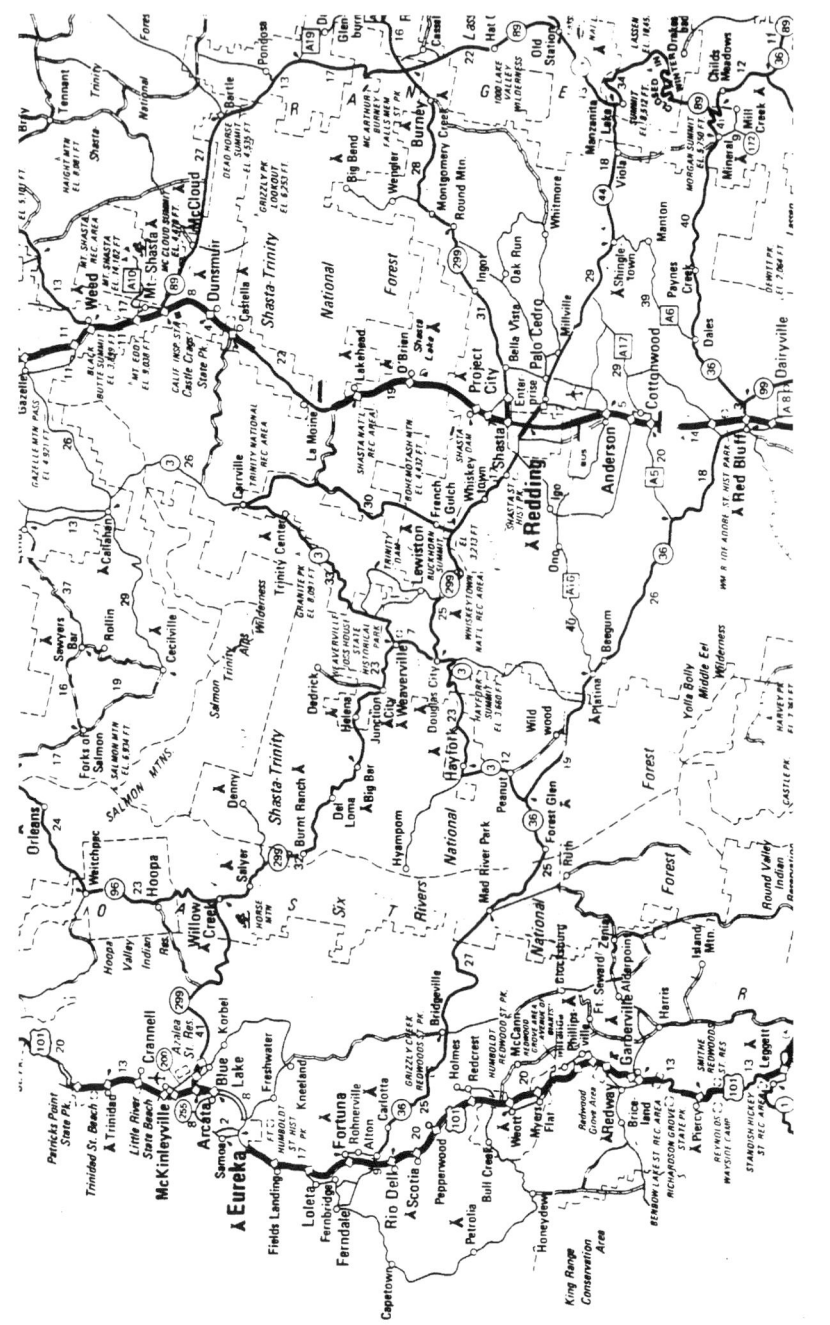

SOMEWHERE OUT THERE

An Englishwoman's Search for her G.I. father

Norma Jean Clarke-McCloud

*To Eleanor & Harry
Best Wishes
Norma Jean Clarke-McCloud
April 2005*

Maka Books
P.O. Box 433, Enfield, EN1 4ZT, U.K.

First published in Great Britain 1998 by
Maka Books
P.O. Box 433, Enfield, EN1 4ZT, U.K.

Reprinted June, 1999
Reprinted January, 2000

British Library Cataloguing-in-Publication Data.
A catalogue record for this book is available
from the British Library.

ISBN: 0-9533749-0-4

© Norma Jean Clarke-McCloud, 1998

Front Cover Photograph by
Mike Lawn, Professional Photographer.

All rights reserved.

Norma Jean Clarke-McCloud asserts her moral right to be identified as the Author of this work in accordance with the Copyright, Designs and Patents Act, 1988.

This book may not be reproduced, in whole or in part, in any form (except by reviewers for the public press), without prior permission in writing from the publishers.

Printed by ***Manuscript ReSearch Printing,***
PO Box 33, Bicester, Oxon, OX6 7PP, U.K.

To my beloved children,
Hayley and ***Adam,***
who shared this great adventure.

ACKNOWLEDGEMENTS

To my father, for being there, for loving me — and for all that *'Sugar'*.

To Harvey, Peter and Mary — my new siblings. Thanks for the warm welcome.

To my Aunt Sandra, for her courage in doing the right thing — with her suggestion about Larry the G.I. soldier.

To my Aunt June — for her help and understanding.

To Pamela Winfield — founder of TRACE and her membership secretary, **Sophia Byrne,** for their solid support.

To Harold Ludwig — my 'helper' in Missouri, for his relentless perseverance that matched my own!

To Philip Grinton — my 'helper' in California, for meeting me in San Francisco!

To Charles Pelligrini — for his help and his compassion.

To Reg Robinson, the researcher at Stansted Airport — for his continued help over the years.

To Shirley McGlade — for taking on the 'might' of the U.S. Military.

To Christine Nicholson — my friend who saw my exhaustion and helped me over my 'final hurdle'.

To Leslie Emery (Uncle Les) — for believing in me.

To all the children conceived in War time and still searching for their father — never give up, whatever you might find at the end.

To everyone who helped and supported me in my quest to find my elusive father — I thank them. I will never forget them.

FOREWORD

The title for SOMEWHERE OUT THERE came about in a very poignant way.

About a month after my Aunt's suggestion that Larry might be my father, I had taken my then two young children to see the Disney film, AMERICAN TAIL. It was about a little mouse who loses his family and searches the whole of America for them. All three of us had been in tears at the happy ending, as eventually and dramatically, they are reunited!

Dabbing at my eyes with a tissue we stood up to leave, just as the haunting song was being played.

"Lets stand at the side and listen to the words of the song?" I turned and whispered to the children.

As I listened to the words, I felt a lump rise up in my throat. Surely these words have been written exclusively for me! I smiled to myself.

The very next day I went out and bought the record. Whenever I would feel defeat taking over during my gruelling seven year search, I often played it.

I would dream of finding my father and think to myself that at least we were both sleeping underneath the same big sky!

I hope that my story will encourage others to never give up, no matter what they may find at the end.

I decided to call my Autobiography, SOMEWHERE OUT THERE—the name of that song.

SOMEWHERE OUT THERE

Somewhere out there, beneath the pale moonlight.
Someone's thinking of me and loving me tonight.
Somewhere out there, someone's saying a prayer,
That we'll find one another in that big somewhere, out there.

And even though I know how very far apart we are it helps to think we might be wishing on the same bright star.

And when the night wind starts to sing a lonesome lullaby, it helps to think we're sleeping underneath the same big sky!

Somewhere out there, if love can see us through, then we'11 be together, SOMEWHERE OUT THERE, out where dreams come true.

Lyrics used by kind permission of MCA Music Ltd. ©1993

CHAPTER 1

"Well I think that Larry's your father."

Little did I know that those words so hastily spoken to me on that grey November day in 1986 were to change my life forever!

My mouth dropped open as I caught my breath. I sank back slowly into the armchair and stared wide-eyed at my Aunt Sandra.

Earlier that day I had decided to visit my mother's youngest sister at her home in Enfield, Middlesex, as I occasionally did.

Now, as I sat in the old familiar armchair, feelings akin to being hit with a sledge-hammer wafted over me and I gripped the arms of the chair until my knuckles were white. I felt stunned, my mind was reeling. Suddenly I thought, of course, why hadn't I realised this before? I gazed at my mother's sister once more and noticed that she had a rather worried look on her face.

A smile spread slowly over my face as it dawned on me, how could I have been so gullible over the years?

There were so many questions going round and round in my head that I was beginning to feel quite dizzy.

I thought back to the past and my turbulent childhood with a cold and distant father, who was often angry. A violently red face with arms flaylying in front of me sprang into my mind. The mental image that it conjured up made me feel extremely uneasy. I rapidly closed my eyes trying to dispel the unhappy memory as quickly as it had come to me.

Suddenly thoughts of my childhood blew over me like a chill wind. My childhood had included my older sister Linda who had died so tragically when I was five. Tears filled my eyes as it began to slowly dawn on me that she was no longer my full sister and that she was their child. I felt a sudden outsider, not belonging to them anymore, really not connected to them. Then just who was I connected to?

Maybe I was being irrational but somehow I had always felt this. I had grown up wondering what was wrong with me, why my 'father' didn't like me.

My childish intuition had always told me that Linda was more loved than I, but somehow I had always accepted it, I had loved her too.

I flinched as I remembered in later years the words he had screamed at me: "It's a pity the best girl had to die!"

His red face contorted with rage.

Until that grey November day in 1986, I had never ever understood why he had screamed those words at me. The very next morning after he had spat those shocking words and with the red imprint of his hand still emblazoned across my chest, I asked my mother: "Was that American soldier my father, Mum?"

I held my breath and prayed that she would say he was.

My mother, looking grim, shook her head and without looking me in the eye, answered,

"NO!"

When I was a small child, perhaps around six or seven, I had been playing a lonely game in my neat but sparse bedroom that I had shared with Linda, when my mother had entered and quickly dropped to one knee in front of me. I felt surprised and being at a similar level to her gazed at her, wondering just what she was going to say to me.

She gently placed her hands on my arms and holding me she said; "During the war Norma, I had a friend who was an American soldier." She let out a breath.

An American soldier? Where was America, was it as far away as the moon? I felt excitement rising in me.

"His name was Larry and he gave me this brass cross." I glanced down at her hands.

"Would you like to keep it, Norma?" She smiled gently at me.

I recalled the excitement. This was the first piece of jewellery I had owned and I smiled warmly as I held out my small hand and took it from her.

I gazed down at this cross, turning it over and over in the palm of my hand. I stared hard at it trying to read the strange writing on it. Joy bubbled up in my throat as I noticed a small engraved heart in the very centre of the cross. I told myself then, that this was a very special treasure and that I would always keep it. Thinking about it that day, thirty-three years later, I knew I did still have that special cross.

That fateful November day had been cold and wet. I had decided to pay a visit to my aunt and after a time the conversation turned to the man that I had always called 'dad'. His indifference had always puzzled me and yet I was his 'only child'. I looked at my aunt as I said, "We have lived in this house for two years and yet he has never been to see it."

I had been made even more aware of this when my daughter Hayley had asked me, "Why has Grandad never been to see our bedrooms, Mummy?"

I felt a deep sadness about this, all my life I had tried to make him like me, to love me.

I could remember back when I was a small child actually

questioning my mother and in a little voice asking, "Mummy why doesn't Daddy like me?"

She replied, "Well, you know, when you were being born in the next room, he sat with his head in his hands and cried because he had wanted a boy."

I remember the feeling of sadness I had then at not being a boy for him, and growing up throughout the years with a sense of worthlessness reinforced time and again by 'dad' himself.

After questioning my mother about my 'father's' attitude towards me, she had used clever 'tactics'. These were clever ways of answering my doubts, almost as if she had rehearsed what questions I might ask in the future, long before they had been thought of or even formed in my own mind.

I sat in my aunt's house that day trying to absorb the momentous idea that she had just suggested.

Clinking noises came to me as I listened to her bustle about in the kitchen making a familiar cup of tea.

I gripped the arms of the chair once more as suddenly began to feel angry, very angry. If this were true about me, why hadn't Mum told me? It seemed, according to my aunt, that everyone had known about this business except for me. This dark secret had been known by aunts, cousins, friends all my life!

Tears filled my eyes. How dare they all know this about me and not tell me! This was *my* life we were talking about! The thought of that really hurt me and to this day still remains one of the hardest things that I have had to bear.

I glanced up as I heard my aunt re-enter the room. She took a few steps towards me her arm out-stretched and handed me a cup of tea. I noticed the worry still etched on her face and my hand shook as I took the steaming cup from her, almost spilling it. I grabbed at a tissue and frantically dabbed at my lap mopping up the drops with a vengeance. Everything seemed unreal. I was no longer the Norma Jean that had such a short time ago walked through my aunt's front door, oblivious to what was about to happen to me. I felt as if I had had an enlightenment, a revelation!

I let out a breath and a sense of happiness wafted over me. I felt a warmth starting from my toes and slowly moving up until my whole body was tingling with excitement. There was nothing wrong with me, I thought, there was actually nothing wrong with me as a person only the circumstances of my birth had made me be treated the way I had. I knew then that this man that I had always called 'dad' was not actually genetically related to me. I let out a sigh, it was a great relief.

Sometimes my mother had not protected me enough from her husband. I would sit petrified at meal times when he was there. Sometimes he would shove his chair back from the table and stand to his full six foot height behind me. He would then grab my shoulders from behind and force them back as I flinched to hide the pain. At these times I would look towards my mother pleading with my eyes for her to help me, but being saddened at her bowed head and her silence.

So many times my mother had not defended me enough against him but she had given me her unfailing love and brought me up to be a very caring person.

I began to realise as I sat there that bleak November day, my mother must have been at her wits end discovering her pregnancy as she already had a small daughter, my half-sister Linda. How desperate she must have been with her husband away serving overseas for at least two years.

Many years later, she told me that she had discovered that 'dad' had enlisted and not been called up as he had told her. At that time of his enlistment she had been pregnant with Linda. The first time that he saw his daughter was when she was around two years old.

Times were extremely hard for all after the war, rationing still continued for several years, and effectively ended in 1953.

I spent a lot of time at my grandmother's house before her death when I was seven years old.

My mother always worked to 'make ends meet' and so I would be taken round to her house to be looked after until my mother collected me. Often this job would be allotted to my youngest aunt, Sandra, who was only six years older than me, and had been born just as World War Two broke out.

I vividly remember walking hand in hand with my two youngest aunts, Jill and Sandra, to the old antiquated corner shop. On one of these visits to the shop, we were stopped suddenly by an acquaintance, probably a neighbour, who said to my aunts, "Is that Larry's child—that Yank's!"

She looked straight at me, stretching out an accusing finger at the same time. I felt uncomfortable and confused. She couldn't be talking about me? I didn't understand, what was Yank? I felt my young aunts' own confusion as they both clasped my hands tighter. We smiled awkwardly and quickly shuffled past the unpleasant woman, and hurried onto the shop.

Arriving breathlessly at the corner shop one of my aunt's produced a buff-coloured ration book.

There one of my aunt's would purchase some corned-beef, egg powder and a small amount of butter or sugar or perhaps both.

All the different smells of the shop wafted all around me as I stood there on my tip-toes trying to peer over the shop counter. Excitement would bubble up in me as I began to dream of being in 'Alladin's Cave' in my small and imaginative mind at that time.

Whilst my aunt's purchases were being made, my eyes would wander round the shop, gazing at the tall glass jars of mouthwatering sweets in front of me. I might have been lucky enough to have a penny or two to spend, and I would choose perhaps some of my favourite liquorice or a sticky lollipop.

There were times though, when I would spend what money I had on cat food for all the stray, straggly cats that hung around my grandmother's back door. I would listen to their pitiful mewing, and unable to bear their hunger, I would often spend what little pocket money I had in that way.

I was about ten years old the next time I heard the American soldier's name of Larry mentioned. I was standing in the doorway of my grandmother's kitchen leaning against the old wooden table. The kitchen was situated at the back of the house and in need of decoration. An old gas boiler on shapely metal legs stood on one side of the room. When my grandmother had been alive I would sometimes help to do the washing in it, watching her lift up the red-hot lid and with the steam billowing all around her she would poke and prod the washing many times until it was clean. After that the wash would be put through an old wooden mangle and I would be instructed to catch the wash as it came through the other side as flat as a board.

Directly to one side of my grandmother's kitchen was a doorway which led into an old bathroom. This bathroom was rarely used and consisted of an old cast-iron bath raised off the ground on metal legs. Directly beside the bath was the sink, the taps of this sink were so stiff to turn on that no one who dwelled there attempted to use them. Washing was mostly done in the kitchen sink at that time.

The toilet was situated outside the house, a few feet from the back door and I hated to have to go on a cold or wet day. This toilet was very pokey with just enough room to manouevre. There was an old wooden seat on the toilet and hanging on a nail beside it were old torn off pieces of newspaper all held together with a piece of string. I would enter the toilet with dread if I needed to use that paper, knowing full well that not only would the print be all over my hands but that it would be all over something else as well!

My mother had lived with my grandmother (her mother) during the war and given birth to my sister Linda in her house. My grandmother had six daughters, but sadly one of the daughters had died at the age of two with meningitis.

Immediately after the war my mother and 'father' were given a prefab to live in by the local council. This was a flat roofed dwelling seemingly made of layers and layers of cardboard. It was just like a detached bungalow, with a nice sized indoor bathroom and the luxury of hot running water, a far cry from my grandmother's house. The kitchen in the prefab was just the right size and it had the added luxury of a 'meat safe', a square box made of wire mesh. This 'meat safe' could be positioned inside or outside the prefab, depending on your preference and the weather. Having a refrigerator was only for rich people in those days.

In the spacious front room there was an open fire which was the only source of heating in the prefab, and in the winter everywhere would be freezing. The job to light the fire was always my 'father's' and I would enter the room with dread, watching as he held up large sheets of newspaper over the fire in an attempt to get it started. The newspaper would cause a vacuum and technically 'draw' the fire up the chimney. This was not always the case as often I would witness the newspaper turning into a flaming fireball with my 'father' shouting in panic as he scrambled madly to put out the flames.

During the winter months my sister and I would have a bath in an old tin bath in front of the open fire. Although it would be very hard and cramped sitting in it, I would look forward to winter bath nights with great excitement.

Thinking back to that day when I was about ten years old and standing in my grandmother's kitchen, I heard Larry's name mentioned again as my attention was drawn to a rather heated row going on in the front room. I quickly turned my head and noticed that the row was between my mother and one of her sisters. A feeling of unease came over me and holding my breath I stepped slowly backwards into the kitchen, hoping that they would not notice my presence there. I stood very still, almost as if I sensed that this had something to do with me?

I jumped as my aunt suddenly sprang out of her chair and snatched an old studio type photo that had been obviously wedged down the side of an old wooden dresser. I peered round the door and froze. My mother's face looked *so* angry. In fact I had never seen her so angry.

"I'll show it to him, I will, I will!" My aunt being an impetuous teenager, yelled!

I felt myself flinch again as my mother moved quickly towards my aunt and lunged at the photo, grabbing it from her and holding it fast!

My mother's speed had obviously surprised my aunt and she let go of the photograph just as suddenly.

For a few moments there was silence and feeling braver now I moved very slowly into the front room. I looked at my mother's face which was much calmer now and with a quivering voice said, "Can I see the photo, Mummy?"

My mother lifted her wistful gaze from the photo and as if she had suddenly remembered that I was there she bent over and handed me her prized possession and said , "Norma, this is the American soldier, Larry, I told you about. Do you remember?"

I gently took the photo from her hands and stared at it. This man was very young and handsome. I noticed that he had a small pipe in his left hand and that he had signed it with 'All my love, Larry'. As I stared at my biological father in his Army uniform the poignancy of the moment was lost on me. I was never to see that photograph again.

Once again thoughts of my childhood blew over me like a chill wind.

My mother and 'father' were always rowing, and with an intuition beyond my years I always sensed that the rows somehow involved me. After the furious arguments a pattern would emerge. They would stop speaking for weeks on end, sometimes as much as eight weeks at a time. During this time I would take on the role of messenger between them. The atmosphere in the house at those times was unbearable, but as usual the same old ritual occurred and my mother was always the one to break the dispute. He would never, ever, give in. After these disputes were over the atmosphere would lift and I would immediately get this feeling of lightness and relief. Invariably I would be bought something, as I presumed in recompense. He would show me a kind of affection, not in hugs or cuddles, but a word or a smile, which I now know was linked to their emotional mood swings and guilt on both their parts, towards me.

I recalled Christmas time as a child, although I loved it there was always a sadness around my mother. I knew she must be missing Linda, as I was, but there was something else wrong, and for all my young years I would sense this and feel uneasy.

On Christmas morning I would lay in my bed and stretch out my toes hoping desperately for a sign that Father Christmas had been. I would clasp my pillowcase and its contents with both hands and within a few minutes my small body was clambering into my mother's bed. My 'father' would immediately leave the room. I would feel confused and disappointed at his annual disappearance, as he rarely watched me open my presents, preferring to retreat downstairs.

"Why does daddy not stay, mummy?"

"Well, he had bad Christmases as a child, he really doesn't like them," she would reply.

From time to time she had related to me the story of my 'father's' Victorian upbringing. He and his siblings had one toy each and they were only allowed to play with them on Christmas day or birthdays.

"He hated Christmas." She said sadly.

The years moved on. I was now nineteen and preparing to marry. The undesirability of continuing to live under my parents roof led me, I now admit, to marry the first boyfriend that I ever had. The first male that had shown me affection. My fiance, Peter, also came from an unhappy homelife. In our naivity we thought we would 'save' each other.

Meanwhile the rows at home continued, sometimes with such an anger, so full of venom. I would lay cocooned in my bed listening to the steady rise of their voices as I tugged the covers over my head, hoping to drown out the noise.

One particular day a heated row was in full flow and once again I took to the sanctity of my bedroom. Suddenly I sat up, I felt alarmed and strained my ears.

I could hear a fearful pleading in my mother's voice. I swung my legs over the edge of the bed and tiptoed across to the door. I was so afraid of what he would do if he caught me eavesdropping, but the pull of trying to help my mother was so strong and I continued to tread stealthily down the stairs. My heart was pounding, I could hear that my mother was actually locked in the cupboard that ran under the stairs. The door rattled and I heard her pleading with him to let her out. I put my hand to my mouth as the silent tears trickled down my face. My mind was racing, how can I help her, what can I do? Suddenly he passed by the kitchen door and I turned and ran back up the stairs ashamed of my cowardice, so afraid I was of him, that I knew that there was nothing that I could do to help her. Breathlessly I reached my room and flung myself sobbing down onto the bed. After a time all was quiet and I sensed that she had been released. The next day nothing was spoken of this to me and yet I knew that I would never be able to erase it from my mind, ever.

My engagement to my boyfriend was imminent. The hall had been booked, the guests had been invited. 'Dad' refused to come. I just could not understand it. Why, I would ask over and over again? It was deeply upsetting and once more I asked myself, how he could do this to me, his only child? Would he have refused to come if it had been Linda's engagement party instead of mine?

My sister, when she was very young, had become very ill with a heart defect. One of her heart valves was faulty and an operation to rectify this was necessary.

"Or she will be in a wheelchair before she's twelve years old!" the doctors told my mother.

Unfortunately in those days there was no such thing as a heart-lung machine. Today, this machine is used in heart operations to simulate the heart whilst the patient's own heart is stopped. The operation on Linda placed a great strain on her still beating heart, and two months after this dramatic operation she became gravely ill. A minute stitch deep within her heart, the size of a pin-head, had begun to leak. I stood beside her and watched Linda as she lay on our mother's big bed. Pain wracked her small body, then suddenly the ambulance came and she was gone, gone from me forever. She had been my ally in my stormy sea, how would I get along without her? I didn't know it then, but this made things far worse for me.

My marriage plans were going ahead and for me I couldn't get away fast enough, and yet I hadn't forseen what my marriage and its plans would mean.

'Dad' did not want to give me away. The knowledge of this hurt me deeply. I couldn't understand why?

I would lay on my bed listening to their rows over it. Once more there was this terrible sadness, why couldn't I have a normal family, a dad that is happy for his daughter, why was this happening to me? I had tried to be a good daughter, one to be proud of, but this never made an impression on him. His thin steely mouth as he looked at me, said it all.

I would question my mother and as usual she had her answer ready, "Well he doesn't want you to get married." She turned away from me.

My mother used to speak of my 'father' questioning my boyfriends suitability. Peter my fiance, had a self employed job, and we were only nineteen and twenty, and yet my 'father' had never expressed these opinions to me at any time. Once again my mother had probably thought out the answers to my puzzling questions on my wedding. Was he punishing my mother through me? I believe that if a 'father' loved a 'daughter', genetically related or not he would do anything to make her wedding day the happiest day of her life!

I left school at fifteen and went straight into a job as a trainee hairdresser. I had always loved fiddling with my friends' hair at school and created Bee-hive hairdo's in the cloakroom. I had already been working as a 'Saturday' girl whilst still at school.

It was really hard work as I was there Wednesdays and Fridays straight from school and then all day Saturdays. Being a hairdressing 'junior' was really hard toil. Often I felt like the general 'dogsbody' doing all the unpleasant tasks around the shop, such as making sure that the shop floor was always swept clean of hair. Keeping the combs, brushes and rollers clean. Cleaning the wash basins in between shampooing the client's hair. At one salon I was even asked to clean the toilets out once a week, I loathed it.

There was always customers who would have to complain about something, but on the other hand there would be the happy cheerful client, who always lightened the salon the moment they stepped inside the door. There was always funny things happening, such as the time when a client had switched her hairdryer off instead of just turning it down, and sat like that for at least thirty-five minutes without realising it, and then couldn't comprehend why her hair was still soaking wet!

One time I worked at a small antiquated salon which still had the old fashioned perming machine. This machine was wheeled into position behind the client and its hood positioned over the client's hair. Then wires from the machine were literally 'plugged' into the perm culers on the customers head. This procedure had to be monitored really carefully or the smell of singeing hair would permeate throughout the salon, resulting in a certain amount of panic, leading to a discreet 'cover-up' by the staff.

At this same salon, occasionally during the lunch hour we would dabble with the Ouiji Board. This is a mystical type of game, where a glass tumbler would be turned upside down on a flat board, surrounded by letters of the alphabet and numbers. These were written on small pieces of paper and placed carefully around the glass. Everyone that was partaking in this had to place the tip of one finger on the glass while questions were asked of a 'spiritual' nature. This was really quite frightening for me at that time, and I felt decidedly nervous about tinkering with the 'spirits' as I had heard that demons could invade the glass itself! It was a good job that the salon was closed for lunch, or 'would be' customers would have heard screams and squeals of laughter as the glass whizzed round and round the make-shift board!

During this time I found my work extremely rewarding in a creative way, but also I found that I would listen to my customers problems and be able to counsel or console them if neccessary. I found great job satisfaction at that time.

It was a few weeks before my wedding and I was working in a hairdresser's just a ten minute walk from my home in Enfield. The salon was very busy and I was occupied in front of the mirror chatting to a client who happened to be my cousin Allen's girlfriend at that time. I combed and teased her fine blond hair, coaxing it into a bouffont shape, and peering at her through the mirror, I began to relate to her about my 'fathers' reluctance to give me away at my wedding. I had found this extremely upsetting to talk about to anyone but I think that day I was hoping that she just might come up with a reason for his reluctance. I was certainly not prepared in any way for her answer.

Her voice rose high above the hairdryer's as she looked back at me, "Well, I've heard that he's not your real dad!"

For a second I stared at her. Had I heard her correctly? My stomach lurched and tears welled up in my eyes and I tried to swallow an enormous lump that had formed in my throat. I recall an awareness of how much my legs ached. I had spent a hard day at the salon and somehow I didn't want to let my upset show at her shocking words about my 'father' not being my 'father'! I tried to stay calm, turning my back for a brief second as I wiped at my eyes. The rest of the day was spent in a dream. I couldn't wait for the last client to go and the shop to finally close. I felt an urgency in the pit of my stomach. I had to get home and tackle Mum with this. Surely it couldn't be true, could it? I asked myself over and over. Finally I helped the last client on with her coat, settled her bill, grabbed my coat and hurried off up the road towards home.

At last the end of the road was in sight and I breathlessly muttered to myself,

"Please, God, don't let him be home yet!"

I knew that if I couldn't speak to my mother about this I would explode inside! My hands were shaking as I fumbled for my door keys in my hurry to get inside the house. I quietly pushed open the door and peered round it. I felt full of dread in case he was there, but in a few moments I knew that Mum and I were alone. I took a deep breath and immediately launched into the revelation that had been revealed to me. After I finished speaking I turned, looked straight at her and said, "Mum, is this true about me? If it is then I want to know." My eyes filled with tears.

With her eyes downcast she replied, "No it isn't."

I suddenly felt a surge of deep anger and began shouting, "Then how dare they say those things about me, things that just aren't true! I don't want them at my wedding!" I put my head in my hands and sobbed.

I lifted my head and watched as mum turned away from me and quietly opened the door and went into the hall. A few seconds later I heard muffled tones on the telephone and knew that she must be phoning our relatives. I braced myself for her raised voice, angry at this terrible lie.

I felt puzzled as I strained my ears for her rage, a rage that never came. But very quickly other thoughts overtook me and I began to prepare myself for the almighty row that would ensue that night, once 'dad' found out that I didn't want them at my wedding. We had always been great friends with this side of the family, and with that I thought no more of my mother's subdued phone call.

Later that same evening I sat quietly in the front room. I knew that I was breathing heavily and my heart was pounding, as I heard mum telling him. I held my breath and stared at the T.V. seeing nothing. I clutched my hands and braced myself for his wrath. Suddenly he was shouting and my stomach lurched. I knew then that we were going to have weeks of silence as the old pattern would follow. I waited and waited for something more to be said about it, but to my surprise no comments were ever made on this subject again.

Looking back now I can understand his anger, his pent up frustration, but nothing can condone his treatment of me as a small child growing up. None of this was my fault, I now tell myself.

Twenty five years later, and although it was a long wait for my estranged relatives and I to meet once again, we are now firmly reconciled. We have talked with regret and sadness about the past, although we understood what happened to us, what severed us as a family so long ago. In the meantime preparations continued for my wedding. I knew that my 'father' had not wanted to be there, and I did not want him to be there. I pressed my mother to ask a favourite uncle, Peter Andrews, to 'give me away' instead.

"I would much prefer it!" I said angrily. But it was not to be as my mother had finally talked her husband into it. He had grudgingly relented. Not that I cared, and in fact I felt very disappointed, but I knew there was nothing that I could do about it. I just looked forward to getting out of my unhappy home as soon as possible.

On my wedding day, the atmosphere was unbearable. Mum

and 'dad' were not talking to one another, and 'dad' was not talking to me. I decided that I could be just as stubborn and just as silent as he was, making my way up the stairs and firmly closing my bedroom door.

On the slow drive to the church not one word passed between us. His face looked grim on all the photographs. He chose not to speak to any of the guests and at the reception upset his sister by telling her to 'clear off'!

It was a tremendous relief to me once the wedding was over and we were on our way to make a new home in Northamptonshire. All I wanted then was to put as many miles between my 'father' and I as possible!

I realise now that I had used an early marriage as a means of escape; in those days it was not the decent thing for a girl to live with a man before marriage.

Two children and twenty years later I had this overwhelming need to return to my roots in Enfield. I always loved to see Mum but the fear of living too near 'dad' had been removed from me as they had now retired to Dorset. Years before my mother had bought a six berth caravan in Dorset, not far from the sea. It was a very beautiful place, and she and 'dad' travelled down most weekends. One day they decided that it would be a lot easier to live there permanently, and so they moved to a property high up on the cliffs.

Now 'dad' has Mum all to himself, I thought to myself at the time.

A few years after we had moved to Northamptonshire my mother followed. She bought a property a short drive from us.

"You can come with me or stay in Enfield, its up to you," she said to him, shrugging her shoulders.

He chose to go with her, not wanting to be on his own. During the years that they were there, Mum's time spent with us was very limited. He was posssessive and when he was at home, he expected her there as well. Sometimes he would telephone our home if she was visiting, and within ten minutes she would grab her coat and bag, and hurry out of the door. During these times I always felt a deep sadness for what 'might have been', always yearning deep down to be part of a happy family.

When my mother moved to Dorset I would make the effort go and visit them once a year. It had hurt me that she could leave me and the children and put such a distance between us. Knowing things as I do now, I can understand her creating this distance between us, the temptation to confess, to tell me the truth was out of her mind.

Our annual visit came round and myself and two very excited children clambered on board the Inter-City train to stay for a week.

After arriving in Dorset and unpacking our cases, the atmosphere in their home was not too bad, but after about three days 'dad' would get into a bad mood. I could never understand why, and yet I really was expecting it at some point during our stay. The old pattern would come into play. More often than not it was about the dinners my mother had prepared. Complaints about her food happened all my life. For some reason, unknown to me, he would get up from the table and stomp out into the kitchen, then I would feel the tension in the air as I gripped my knife and fork tightly. Inevitably I would hear the scraping of a perfectly nice meal that my mother had just cooked, being dumped straight into the bin! When I was a child it was very different. Then the dinners would be flung up the walls with a vengeance!

After one such scene a relative, Ann, arrived to find my

mother up the stepladder, tears raining down her face, frantically scrubbing his dinner from the ceiling.

Those times spent with my mother in Dorset were precious to me. We strolled the lush green hills whilst taking the children on nature trails and enjoying each other's company. As we ambled along the narrow cliff pathways stopping from time to time to enjoy the spectacular views, we would talk and talk. I could sense that she was dreadfully unhappy but as usual I felt powerless to help her and she seemed unable to help herself. Twenty years previous to our annual visit to the shores of Dorset, mum had left 'dad' albeit briefly, and in a flurry of madness she had returned to him. I had always felt that she had made a big mistake.

I thought about the few times mum managed to visit us. It was usually planned around the children's birthdays. She would always come alone. She would make the long journey in her old, battered green car, so afraid that it would let her down on the way. The children would get very excited at her visits and would sit with their noses pressed against the window, waiting for her arrival. I knew that she loved visiting us as much as we loved having her, but as the days went by I could see the worry draw over her face like a transparent veil. 'Dads' possession of my mother was all consuming. He did not like her to go anywhere without him. After her visit he would end up sulking and not speaking to her for days.

I used to feel puzzled as to why he had never been to see our house. After all I was daughter to both of them, or so I used to think.

Mum being with us just for a few days was all that I could hope for.

"Look I'd better be going back soon, you know what he's like. Anyway he's all alone there. What if he had an accident or something?"

I would look at her and shrug my shoulders.

I wonder if they are his words or yours, I would think to myself.

I answered her, "Well that's up to you Mum," and felt a sadness inside. Why does she always put him before me?

Nobody had to tell me about that kind of brainwashing. I saw it as Victorian brainwashing. 'Women are only there to look after the men' type of attitude. This attitude of the men being the boss and the woman being the servant to the family, was very predominant during the reign of Queen Victoria. This attitude is still very much in evidence from the generation of the World War Two era. Some would say that this mental view is still carried on in some families today.

Suddenly a voice came to my ears. Where was I? I glanced across the room, and with the feelings of being catapaulted back to the present, I became aware that it was my Aunt Sandra's voice that I could hear. I realised that I was still sitting in her comfortable armchair, and the revelation of what had been suggested to me about the American Soldier called Larry, wafted over me once more.

"Why don't you write and ask your mother about Larry?" My aunt smiled.

"Yes," my voice cracked.

"Yes, yes I will," I grinned.

I thought to myself, for God's sake, here I am forty years old! I'm not the person that I always thought I was. Then who the HELL am I?

Later as I sat in my car waving goodbye to my aunt, I stared around me feeling so different. The day although still very grey seemed brighter. The whole world had taken on a different perspective to me.

As a child growing up even right up to now, I had felt so

different. Now I knew what I was going to have to do. I would have to find out the truth one way or another and if it was true then I would search for this Larry for better or for worse, whatever I might find at the end.

CHAPTER 2

Mum and I always telephoned each other twice a week. I phoned her on Sundays and she phoned me on a Wednesday. Since she had moved to Dorset from Northamptonshire, we had missed each other's company very much. Telephoning each other regularly kept us close even though we lived so far apart.

I was still reeling from the conversation that I had had with my aunt the day before. I was still feeling numb and walked about my house in a dream. Was this really true? I asked myself. My thoughts kept returning to the idea that there was only one way to find out the truth and that was to ask my mother. I had to approach her and yet I knew her well enough to know that she would be dreadfully upset. My stomach turned over at the thought of it.

If it was true then my mother had lied to me all my life, I couldn't believe that she would do such a thing to me! I loved her so much. If it was true then she had known that others had this knowledge about me. I felt sick at the thought. If my 'father' wasn't my father, why had she kept it from me, why had she lied? She had betrayed me. Wasn't I important enough to her, for her to consider my feelings? I paced round and round the front room, sitting down briefly and then jumping up to pace round the room once more.

I knew that asking her was going to be really hard but I could see no way round it, I had to know.

After all, this was *my* life we were talking about, not my mother's. She had acted as if it were nothing to do with me. I swallowed hard, frowning. I would never be able to understand her reasoning, especially after I was married and moved so far away from them.

Maybe, I thought, she hadn't wanted to tell me because it would have caused even more trouble between her husband and herself. All I could think of was that she had been grossly unfair to me.

I looked at myself in the mirror. Maybe I had a father somewhere, a father who was kind and loving. Maybe I still had a genetic father and suddenly I thought, he could still be alive! I felt excitment rise in me, then a doubt crept into my mind. I had lived for forty years thinking that 'dad' was my father. I knew then that I would need absolute confirmation from my mother. I needed to actually hear her say 'yes' it is true, although deep down in my inner-self I already knew that it was true.

That night once the children were in bed, I made myself a hot chocolate and sat down quietly. I needed to think about my options. How on earth was I going to tackle Mum? If I telephoned her he could be listening to our conversation from the next room. Well, he wouldn't be able to hear my questions but he would hear the shock in her voice. 'Dad' was always very strict about her using the telephone and whilst she was using it he would prowl back and forth like a lion, making her feel so uncomfortable that she would quickly replace the receiver. In the end I decided against phoning her, it was no good I thought, it would have to be a letter. I tried to put myself in her position, at least then she could choose how to tell me. I knew that I would not actually be seeing her for several months, and I was bursting inside to know the truth. I got up and went to my bureau, retrieved pad and pen and sat down at the table and began to write. It was to be one of the hardest letters I have ever written. That night I wrote and re-wrote that letter. I had to get the words just right. I was very conscious of her feelings and I tried to write it so that it wouldn't hurt her too much, realising at the same time that I had no idea what her reaction would be. One thing that I was really sure of was that she would protect 'dad' first as she always did.

I heaved a great sigh as finally I inserted the letter into its envelope and placed it on the mantlepiece ready for posting the next day. Once it was posted I knew that I was just going to have to wait for her reply. Time ticked away like the ticking of a time-bomb. I knew that I was waiting for some sort of reaction. I tried very hard to think optimistically. Mum would telephone at her usual time and we'd have this very pleasant conversation in which she would confess everything to me. After which she would be extremely happy to divulge my Father's name and as a bonus, where he came from. I smiled at the thought of it being as easy as that! In reality I was to be very badly mistaken about finding out the truth connected to Larry the American soldier.

At last, Wednesday, the day my mother usually phoned, arrived. I kept myself busy working around the house, feeling sick with my stomach in knots. Every time the phone rang I jumped, but as the time went on a distinct feeling of unease came over me as my mother's phone call never came! I felt so shocked! I knew that Mum loved me very much and I couldn't believe that she wouldn't telephone me at the allotted time. After all we had been doing this for years, I thought to myself. Maybe she's ill or maybe she's forgotten what day it is?

The omission of her call stunned me and yet at the same time it spoke reams!

A few days passed by and still no phone call. It was now

Sunday, my day to telephone. I still had no word from my mother. Surely if it wasn't true she would have called me at her usual time and been very angry at my letter.

I decided to be still and do nothing.

Another week passed by and with only thoughts of my mother inside my head, suddenly the telephone rang. My heart leapt into my mouth, could this be Mum? I thought, as I tentatively picked up the receiver.

"Hello",

"Norma!" it was a very grim sounding Mum.

"Yes," I flinched.

"How dare you write a letter like that to me!"

She sounded really angry. I opened my mouth to speak.

"Of course your father is your father!" She almost spat at me.

Tears pricked at my eyes as I felt like a little girl once more. She was speaking as if she had rehearsed her lines over and over.

"He registered you when you were six weeks old, do you think that he would have done that if you weren't his!" Her voice was rising.

I replied meekly,

"Maybe he didn't know then?" I felt myself shrinking and paled as I thought I had never heard my mother so angry with me in all my life! Not even when I was a little girl.

I tried to explain in the ensuing conversation who had suggested this and my reasons for believing it, but as I talked I knew that there was not much point. I tried to justify my letter but it was almost as if she totally convinced herself over the years that her husband was my father. After all she had 'eaten', 'drunk', and 'slept' this lie for over forty years, maybe she did really think that it was true.

I felt a deep sadness as a few moments later we ended the conversation and said goodbye. As I replaced the receiver and with shoulders hunched I moved towards the lounge knowing full well that she was lying. I had always trusted my mother, I never believed that she would ever lie to me. A tear trickled down my face and grabbing a tissue, I wiped it away. That day on the telephone my trust in her flowed away like water down the drain.

Mum and I had always got along well although we'd had our moments as all mums with daughters will tell you, but we had a closeness that some would envy. Why couldn't she open up to me now? I wasn't a child, I was forty years old! My mother's father had died when she was twelve. He had been a steam-train driver earning three shillings a week, a very good wage in those days. They had lived extremely well, with her father always carving things out of wood. Garden furniture and special toys were lovingly created for his young family. My mother remembered with affection a splendid rocking horse, with a real horse-hair mane and tail, but most of all she remembered the large red engine that he made, which was big enough to sit on and had brought endless joy to my mother and her twin sisters.

When her father died suddenly through a brain tumour, they were plunged into poverty. There wasn't a welfare state then and everything her father had made so lovingly, had to be burnt on their open fire during the winter, to stop them from freezing.

With a lump in my throat I thought about my mother at least knowing her father, she knew what he looked like, she knew his name. He had held her lovingly in his arms. I had never been given this chance in all the years. I thought how my mother knew her sisters and all their names, I might have another sister somewhere? Why couldn't my mother put herself in my position, as I tried to put myself in hers? If this were true and I wasn't her husband's child, she must have been frantic with worry. Her husband was away in India, he had yet to see the child of their marriage. I thought about how young she was, only twenty-one, how alone and afraid she must have felt not knowing if her husband would return from the war alive.

My mother was fifteen when the war broke out. All her youth was taken up with war. From time to time she had related to me about the terrible bombings on London. I could imagine the excruciating fear that people must have felt as the doodle-bugs dropped all around them night after night. I visualised people crouched in the underground stations or shelters listening desperately to the drone of the doodle-bugs engine, bracing themselves for the silence, and the waiting as the bomb dropped on its target below.

I imagined people throwing themselves under anything that could afford them some kind of protection and there, as they crouched in the darkness, the sweat would ooze from every part of their bodies. They would hug their children to them or clasp their hands praying to their particular God. They would hold their breath and brace their bodies wondering if the bomb would land on them this time.

Then to try to sleep in a cold dank Anderson shelter. These were bomb shelters named after John Anderson who was the Lord Privy Seal at that time. The shelters were issued to householders during World War two. Made of corrugated iron, they were sunk deep into the ground in the majority of the nation's gardens, where some remain even to this day.

The British Government had issued these shelters along with gas masks in order to afford the population some kind of protection from the enemy. When the wail of the sirens started, people would rush to go down into the shelters and wait expectantly until the 'all clear' siren sounded.

Many people abused this safety, preferring to take a risk and stay in the comfort of their own homes.

My mother once laughingly related to me, that she and 'dad' would do their 'courting' with the shrapnel dropping all around them!

"We never knew fear in those days," she commented.

During those war years everyone was always hungry. I thought of my mother having to tolerate food rationing, for years never tasting a banana, only seeing pictures of them in books. All my mother's teenage years were filled with deprivation. She married at seventeen and had given birth to my sister as the bombs reigned down on London. When Linda was six weeks old a bomb dropped in a street behind their house, totally destroying everything and everyone who lived there. My mother awoke to find her sister June, her body covered in glass, as she lay across Linda to protect her.

Then suddenly one day at the end of a long and weary war full of such hardships, she met an American soldier. He was a bearer of wonderful gifts. This kind and generous affectionate American brought a bright light into my mother's dreary world. He hauled a large wooden box over her threshold, made by a prisoner of war, and gave it to my mother. This box was full of 'hard to get' things, especially those prized silk stockings. My father had given this to my over-joyed mother and she being so deprived, accepted it gladly. As for my mother, she fell in love with the kind and handsome soldier. No wonder the inevitable happened. Put to the test anyone who found warmth in the coldness of war would find the companionship hard to resist.

I cannot remember how or when, but I had always known that my mother met Larry through her sister June. My aunt June had met Carl Wraley another G.I. and eventually married him.

Larry was his buddie. I knew that my uncle Carl had been stationed at Stansted Airport, near Bishops Stortford in Essex, England, during World War Two.

Stansted was about half an hour from where the two sisters lived at that time. I had always believed that Carl had brought Larry home to meet his wife's family and finding that they all got along so well, they made up a foursome.

As soon as the war was over June made plans to take herself and her baby son, Gary, for a reunion with Carl who by then had been repatriated. Her mother was broken hearted when June left taking her baby grandson away from her, she sobbed fearing that she would never see either of them again.

In those days of deprivation, if you ever reached American soil you never returned. There were no cheap Atlantic flights, most of the travel was by boat. The expense to return home would be way out of most people's reach. It was twenty years later when my aunt stepped back onto British soil and her mother's premonition sadly came true. June never saw her mother alive again.

Meanwhile it was now Christmas 1986. At last we had moved back to my roots in Enfield, Middlesex, and I was caught up in all the excitement of hanging tinsel and wrapping Christmas presents with my children, Hayley and Adam. We had the added excitement that mum was visiting us for three days and apart from being good fun she helped out a lot and eased the preparations for me.

At times when I thought about her arrival a part of me would really look forward to it, but the other part would fill me with dread. There wasn't a day that went by without me thinking of this dubious situation in my life. It was so frustrating not to know the absolute truth that sometimes I felt like screaming at her, but an inner feeling always told me it would do no good. I would go over and over my past and my childhood. It made me feel angry as it all made such sense to me now. This was my business not anyone else's. Not even my mother's, no this is my life and I had the absolute right to know all about it. At times I thought about my mother's angry phone call and I feared a repetition. It would be dreadful to ruin our Christmas.

Finally my mother arrived. It was the first time that we had met after that horrendous telephone call. I opened the door and hugged her to me, and knew that we were going to be alright. We carried on as if the subject of Larry the American G.I. had never been broached. We laughed and joked our way through the festive season, and yet I felt it was all still there hanging over us like a dark cloud before a storm. I felt a tightness inside, dying to bring the subject up again, but managed to keep my lips sealed, to hold onto all the questions that I so desperately wanted to ask her. Mum must have been on tender-hooks, nervous and wondering whether I might mention it again?

That Christmas Eve, Mum suggested that she babysat while we went out for a short while. I stared back at her, it was such a surprise as we rarely managed to go out, and she lived so far away that she never babysat. Jumping at the chance for an evening out, we hastily got ready and hurried out the door. On our return I stepped into the front room and my eyes were drawn to an empty bottle standing on the hearth. I looked at my mother and gasped, it was obvious to me that she'd drunk a whole bottle of wine. I didn't know whether to laugh or cry. I felt anxious for her and a deep sadness as something told me that this was linked to Larry and her being untruthful to me. For a second I felt so sad for the sacrifices she must have made in her past and how such a spirited woman had been so suppressed by it.

I linked my arm around my mother and Peter (my then, husband) and I managed to walk her out into the hall. I turned and balancing mum on the first step, I positioned myself behind her and started to push her up the stairs. Suddenly I began to see the funny side of the situation and started to giggle, can this really be happening, it's like a kind of 'farce', a comedy play! Later, after a lot of puffing and blowing and in an undignified manner, I finally heaved my mother into bed!

Facing me the next morning, she said, "Well, you never expected to see me like that, did you?"

We both laughed, and yet for the fear of another angry denial, I just couldn't bring myself to talk of my father again. Thinking back to that time now, I wonder, if I had questioned her, would she have been forthcoming?

Christmas passed by and my mother returned to her home. Months went by and at times I felt as if I should go mad if I didn't find out the truth about Larry, one way or another.

Then suddenly one day, a rush of inspiration came over me. Why don't I go to an Adoption counsellor? I knew about this option, because our children were themselves, adopted. After many years of fertility treatment, involving operations for ovarian cysts and a blocked bowel, and at times plunging to the depths of despair, we were able to put all the heartache behind us with our specially 'chosen' family.

Unknown to me then, wasn't my own situation similar? I asked myself. I had the man that I had always called 'dad' on my birth-certificate, but maybe a counsellor could still listen to me, and make some kind of decision for me, at least give me their opinion as to whether they felt it was true or not. With those thoughts I rushed out into the hall and grabbing the telephone directory, flicked through the pages, and dialled the number. Just as quickly I found myself talking to a social worker. I blurted out my story, feeling rather foolish, realising that I probably wasn't making much sense. It all seemed far-fetched to me let alone a stranger. We made an appointment for the following week, and my stomach turned over at the thought of it. As the time of my appointment came nearer, I began to make excuses not to go. Mum would not like me talking to strangers about this, and if 'dad' found out he'd be so angry! I knew that I was always carrying my parents thoughts and feelings with me. I was always doing what they would be happy about, so desperate for their approval, still a little girl inside. After years of 'put-downs' I just didn't think that I deserved happiness.

It was the day of my appointment at the Civic Centre in Enfield. My stomach was churning as I made my way to the Adoption and Fostering department. I felt anxious. I had the premonition that this meeting was going to drastically change my life. At long last I sat opposite my counsellor and as I opened my mouth to start speaking about my life, a wave of guilt flooded over me. Silently I thought, what if I'm wrong about this, what if my aunt was wrong? Finally I sat back in my chair exhausted. I had given the counsellor all the relevant information along with the fact that my mother had said that I was born prematurely and yet thinking about it my actual weight had been seven pounds four ounces. I had never thought about it before. Over the years I had heard other facts, snippets of gossip, but I had never connected it to myself. When I had challenged my mother on hearing this gossip she had always answered with a very clear but curt 'NO', and I believed her implicitly.

I sat opposite the social worker that day, searching her face, wondering what she thought about the account of my life. For a few seconds I held my breath. She lent back in her chair and smiled at me, "Of course it's true my dear."

I exhaled, hardly daring to believe that I'd actually heard her say those words! "But now you are in charge of your life."

I felt stunned as I looked at her.

"You know as much now as anyone else. You must forget about your mother and her husband. After all, they have chosen the way they want to live and you must get on with your own life." I stared back at her.

How true, I thought. Why had I never looked at it that way before? She pushed her chair away from the desk and stood up.

"If you'll just hang on for a moment I'll go and get the address for the American Embassy, maybe they can help you somehow." She smiled and went out of the room. For a few moments I sat silently stunned. I stared around the room trying to absorb what had been said to me. I shook my head. I didn't believe it! So it wasn't all my imagination. My aunt had been right and my mother had lied.

Shortly the social worker returned and handed me a slip of paper containing the address of the American Embassy on it. I stood up and took it from her, thanked her profusely and turned and went out of the room.

I made my way down in the lift in a kind of fog and out into the busy street in a dream. I knew that once again I was feeling so different. There was a tightness in the pit of my stomach, and yet I felt so excited! At last someone had actually confirmed to me what deep down I already knew, but to have it actually voiced by someone who was totally unbiased was wonderful!

I had to stop thinking about my mother and her husband, the man I'd always called 'dad', and for once in my life think about what I actually wanted. I felt elated! Slowly it began to sink in that 'dad' was really my step-father. I made up my mind there and then that he would have no hold on me anymore.

As I made my way home I told myself that I would have to

search for this Larry if it took the rest of my life to do it. This man was my biological father, and if he were no longer living then I would search for any siblings I might have. Once again I asked myself, what did he look like? Did I resemble him? I knew that I did not have my mother's eyes, so maybe I had his?

I thought about this gaping hole in my life left by the death of my dear sister. Maybe I had another sister somewhere? It was all so intriguing, and I would have to find out somehow. I would leave no stone unturned until I found the other half of my genetic make-up. I would never let it beat me! I must have no regrets!

CHAPTER 3

It was January 1988 when I received a reply from the American Embassy. As I began to tear open the envelope, a part of me still couldn't quite take in the fact that I was actually half-American. In a sense the American Embassy was a part of me.

I thought about my heritage every day, and a deep sadness would sweep over me, as I thought about my mother and her refusal to tell me the truth. In the end I resigned myself to that fact, and after visiting the adoption counsellor, I resolved that I would just have to 'go it alone' and just get on with it! I knew that I would search for this Larry, if it was going to take the rest of my life to do it!

I eased myself back in the armchair and slowly unfolded the letter. The American Embassy had enclosed some very interesting information on how to locate a missing person. At the very bottom of the letter was the name of an organization called T.R.A.C.E. Transatlantic Childrens Enterprise, founded by Pamela Winfield. I read with excitement that this organization help and support G.I. children to find their fathers.

I felt emotionally moved by that letter, that there were others like me and that I was not alone. I set about writing to Pamela Winfield and T.R.A.C.E. immediately.

In a matter of days I had received Pamela's reply, and I realise now that I had some sort of fairy tale notion about Pamela and her membership secretary, Sophia Byrne, believing that somehow they would wave a 'magic wand', look up a few American states for me and 'voilà' there would be my father! He would be waiting eagerly to greet me with his arms outstretched. All this would happen in a few short weeks and then we would all live 'happily ever after'!

Little did I know then what a high mountain I would have to climb. I should have known really, as nothing in my life has ever come easy to me.

On reading the letter from T.R.A.C.E., it was explained that they could advise people on different routes to take, but it was actually routes that I myself would have to try. T.R.A.C.E. could only point me in the right direction. Their last newsletter was enclosed and I began to read it eagerly, finding it very informative. I felt a warmth inside as once more I realised that there were many, many people in the same 'boat' as I. In the beginning I had felt so terribly alone and vastly different from anyone else.

I received TRACE'S newsletters throughout the years of my search, and drew great comfort from them. I would often wait eagerly for them to drop through the letterbox as the time for their distribution came round once more.

I sat back realizing that I had to form some kind of plan, some kind of idea of what to do, but where on earth am I going to start? I asked myself.

I picked up my note pad and pen and heaved a great sigh, I felt so downhearted. I had hoped to make a list of clues that might help me, but I really didn't have much to write down. The only thing that I had as concrete evidence was the name of Larry. The large photo of Larry that had been snatched from behind my grandmother's old dresser formed in my mind. I could vividly 'see' the signature. I remembered it said, 'All my love Larry'. I thought deeper and remembered that the stroke of the 'L' was a sweeping one. I frowned as I began to think about the name of Larry. I wondered what Larry was short for. I am a very romantic person and my imagination drifted off as I visualized Lawrence of Arabia, galloping across the desert on a camel! I decided that I really liked that name, it was such a strong name. I secretly hoped that if Larry had a full name, that it would be that.

If only my uncle Carl were still alive, I sighed. My aunt June's husband had passed away two years before, before I knew of my father. I was beginning to feel depressed. Everything was against me!

I thought about Carl. He was in the eighth Army/Airforce and had been stationed at Stansted airport, Essex, England, during the 2nd World War.

Someone had mentioned this years before and it had stayed on the 'backburner' of my mind. Surely, I thought, if Larry and Carl were buddies, then my father must have been in the same unit, at the same airfield, around the same time. I felt a bit better. I hastily jotted down those facts on my note pad, then I read the facts that I had written, out loud to myself, these were all the clues that I had;

I had the name of Larry, Eighth Army/Airforce and Stansted. It wasn't an awful lot, but it was a start.

Later that same night, it suddenly came to me, that in order to find this man, I would have to write in every direction that I could, and as often as I could. Deep down inside me there was this little niggle about not actually having a surname, but I pushed that fact firmly to the back of my mind.

I walked towards the bureau and retrieved my T.R.A.C.E. newsletter from it. I could remember that there was an address for the Eighth Army. I flicked over the page and I was right, there was one in Florida and one in Essex, England. I decided it would be best to write to both at once then, at the same time, an idea began to form in my mind, surely my father's name must be on a list somewhere here in the U.K. and in the U.S.A. If my uncle Carl's name is on a list of serving men during World War Two, then wouldn't Larry's be there on that list, also?

After I posted the letters, I tried to put them out of my mind, and continue as usual. At that particular time I worked as a supervisory assistant in a local school. I found this convenient as it fitted in with the children's school hours enabling me to take them and meet them from school, which the children and I enjoyed so much. My life was very hectic as not only did I do all household chores, but the gardening, decorating and walking the dog, were also on my daily agenda.

In amongst my very hectic life, suddenly there on the doormat were my two eagerly awaited replies from the Eighth Army. As I read both letters, I heard myself inwardly groan, realising deep down that I had to have Larry's surname or I'd never be able to find him. Both replies asked for much more detail, especially the surname. I felt so disheartened and yet I had only just begun. With a sinking feeling I knew that in reality I was 'clutching at straws'. Mentally I questioned myself. How could I possibly find one man called Larry in the whole vastness of the United States, it was ridiculous really! Even if I did have his surname, I still had no idea where he came from.

As time went on I would try to think of new ways to find my father. Then one day, I had a flash of inspiration. I have a Godmother somewhere, why hadn't I thought about her? She was my mother's best friend when they were young. I had not seen her for over twenty years. It took me a while to remember her name, yes, it was Phyllis, but I had no idea at all of her surname. I could remember her maiden name, but not her married name, so that wouldn't be much good.

After this train of thought I decided to get some fresh air and walk my dog. Maybe a good walk will blow away the 'cobwebs' in my mind, I thought.

Lost in my thoughts, I passed by a neighbour, Jack, also walking his dog, suddenly I remembered that he had lived next door to my Godmother when they were children. How uncanny, I thought, that I should bump into him at this time. That's very strange. I turned and quickly asked him if he remembered Phyllis. For a few seconds he just looked at me, and I held my breath. I looked at him, as suddenly he smiled, and spoke her name, proceeding to tell me about their childhood. I let out my breath, feeling so relieved. I felt like flinging my arms around this elderly gentleman's neck, but thought better of it and stayed calm, as my reasons for wanting this information were strictly secret. After all I wasn't supposed to know about my 'father' not being my father, was I?

My mother and Phyllis had met at school, and were best friends all through their growing up years, until they were adults. My mother had told me that they were always very close. I remember Phyllis from my childhood and her presence in my life. The last time I saw her was just before my marriage. She was around my mother during the war years, surely mum must have taken Phyllis into her confidence. If anyone would know my father's name, she would.

I hurried home from work that day with only these thoughts on my mind. I opened the front door and made straight for the telephone directory. As I ran my finger down the list of names, the palms of my hands were sweating. I couldn't see her name. I felt panic rising in me. It had to be there. What if it was ex-directory? No, I sighed with relief, there it was, thank God!

I picked up the phone and started to dial the number, all the time thinking about what I was going to say to a woman who I hadn't met for years and years. At first there was no answer, but the second time I dialled, she picked up the telephone.

"Hello is that Phyllis?" I felt so nervous.

"Yes, it is." She sounded so different.

I felt awkward as I began to explain to her who I was and asked if I could visit her sometime. I didn't want to go into details over the telephone, after all this was a very delicate matter. I realised that to someone of Phyllis's generation, it would be a shocking thing to have happened.

She sounded really pleased to hear from me, and it was arranged for me to visit her the following week. The time for my visit soon came round and I was driving to meet her. I felt extremely nervous and aware that everything that I wanted to know about my father hung on my visit. Questions went round and round in my mind. What if she did not like me asking her about this, especially if she still felt a strong loyalty to my mother? Maybe my mother had primed her years ago not to tell me, should I ever approach her. I began to think that maybe I really shouldn't be doing this. What would mum say if she found out?

I pulled up outside her ground floor flat, and with my heart in my mouth, I rang her doorbell. Suddenly the door opened and there stood Phyllis, looking so different. I suppose because to me I had always remembered her so dark haired, and the passing of the years had changed her hair colour to a slate grey. The vision that I had as a child, of Phyllis, was tall and slim, and yet now as I stood face to face with my Godmother she seemed only slightly taller and quite a bit stockier than the memory I had of her. She held out her hand and suddenly with the sound of her voice, recollections of Phyllis came flooding into my mind.

I stepped into her neat and tidy home and felt more relaxed

as she turned to fill the kettle in readiness for a cup of tea. As she bustled about I sensed that she was puzzled as to why I had come to see her, and so I decided that I would get straight to the point.

I took a deep breath,

"Phyllis, I have just found out that 'dad' isn't my father and that my biological father was a G.I. soldier. I want to trace him, but I don't know his surname, do you know?" I looked straight at her, silently praying for good news.

With a very puzzled look, she said, "Why no Norma, I never even knew that you had an American father." My heart sank!

"Your mum and I saw each other a lot less once she married and had your sister. I was so busy working."

I was so disappointed. I felt a lump in my throat. I swallowed quickly, I didn't want her to see me cry. I had pinned so many hopes on her. I'd thought about this every day, feeling sure that my Godmother would be able to help me. Now my hopes were dashed! I knew that I would have to think of another way, but one thing that pleased me was that after all those years, I had met my Godmother once more.

Shortly after this happened I received a letter from my aunt June, who lived in Florida. I felt quite excited as she wrote that she would be coming to England and hoped that we would meet up at some point. My spirits rose as I thought, why don't I speak to her about Larry? After all she actually met my father.

I felt a pang. She, surely, would remember his full name and where he came from. I felt excited about the future, and looked forward to her coming, but then doubts crept into my mind. If she did know, would she actually divulge them to me? This information would be against my mother's wishes and my mother being the eldest, the other sisters tended to do as she said. I sighed, determination taking over. Well, I would give it a try.

As time went on, I tried to think of a plan. I thought about each of my mother's four sisters, living far apart in different parts of the country. My aunt Sandra lived quite near me, at that time, in Enfield. Then there was my aunt Jill in Essex and aunt Joan, who lived at that time in Hampshire. My aunt June lived in Florida, she was the twin sister of Joan. Thinking about my mother and her sisters, I knew that I would have to isolate June somehow, take her to one side and speak to her in private. But how, I asked myself?

I had met my aunt June on the occasions that she paid a visit to England, but when I thought about these visits, I had never actually been alone with her. It was something that never crossed my mind before, but now, it slowly dawned on me that maybe my mother had arranged things that way when June visited from the States. Perhaps my mother was afraid that at some point June might divulge my parentage to me and 'let the cat out of the bag'! My thoughts consumed me as I tried to work out how I could be alone with her?

Of course I could understand my aunt's loyalties, her allegiance would obviously lie with her sister, my mother.

At last, my aunt June arrived, and my mother met her and they went to stay in Dorset. After a time she was then going to make her way to Enfield, to stay with Sandra, who lived there at that time. I knew that once June arrived in Enfield, I had to approach her. I felt edgy at the thought of confronting her, and prayed that she would see my point of view, and how unfair the situation was.

A few days later, my telephone rang. My stomach went over as I realised that it was aunt Sandra. She had been the one to suggest to me that Larry might be my father, and I felt that she was on my 'side'. We spoke quickly and in low tones, so that my aunt June would not hear our collaboration.

"Norma, June wants to go and see and old school friend, Pat, who lives in Edmonton. I've suggested that you could possibly give them a lift there?" she whispered.

I knew that Joan her twin would be opposed to my questioning June, and I knew that Joan was with her. That's just too bad, I thought. I felt an overwhelming gratitude towards Sandra at that time, thinking that at least someone was trying to help me.

I looked at my watch, the time had come at last for me to collect my aunts and take them to Edmonton. I felt my stomach tighten, something was driving me, urging me to do this. I had to find out as much information on this Larry as I could, no matter what trouble this might cause in the family. I had to be 'healthily selfish' this was my life! I had to know the truth! That day I had walked around in a daze, rehearsing my words like lines in a play. I prayed to God that my aunt June would live up to my wishful expectations, that she would reply to my questions honestly. Suddenly a wave of anxiety swept over me, what if she says no! What if she said that she wouldn't help me! I quickly pushed those thoughts out of my mind. I knew that if June would not speak to me about Larry then I was going to have to get really firm with her, after all this might be my only chance, I might not see her again for years. I had to corner her, I had to face her head-on!

I pulled up the car and watched my aunts as they walked towards me. I waved to my aunt Sandra, standing nervously at her door and wondered what the outcome would be as I drove back later that night.

Pat, was an old school friend of my aunt's, and they hadn't met for many years. The meeting with her at her flat had been arranged on June's arrival from America. Later I sat nervously on Pat's settee listening to their laughter as they reminisced about their school days and the war years. I knew, as I sat there, that I was physically participating, but mentally I was rehearsing my lines over and over. By the time we came to leave I was a nervous wreck! This was a taboo subject, one that had been buried for over forty years. My mother was a very spirited woman, and yet I had realised that she had been suppressed by her burden of guilt that she carried surrounding my birth. She had been suppressed by her husband, perhaps living in fear of him that he might, in his pent up anger, blurt out her secret to me. Was this why he had had such control over my mother? This control of her was was something that had always puzzled me. She had lived a lie all her life, she had not been true to herself and she had not been true to me. Sometimes I felt that all this really had nothing to do with me at all, it seemed so unreal.

Finally the evening was over and I was driving my aunts back to my aunt Sandra's house. I said to myself, well, this is it, it's now or never! I pulled up and before June and Joan could alight from the car, I took a deep breath and turned round to face my aunts in the semi-darkness. I mustered all my wits and blurted out,

"June, I expect that you know already what I want to talk to you about?" I let out a breath, thinking, there, I've said it at last!

"I think so," she said softly.

I noticed both sisters fidgeting uncomfortably and I felt uneasy.

"June, tell me about Carl's friend, Larry. I know that he is my father." I was feeling extremely brave now, and gripped the steering wheel, as I turned to face the front.

For a split second there was silence, and I held my breath as I waited expectantly for her answer.

"Sure, Larry's your father." I couldn't believe that I had heard correctly. I turned once more to face her.

"My Carl introduced him to your mum." I exhaled as I realised that she was very happy to tell me the truth at last.

"I told your mum years ago that she should tell you. It was your right to know this." She smiled.

Her sister, Joan, as I knew she would be, was silent. I grinned, as relief flooded through me! Here was my aunt June, another sister on my 'side' another ally, an ally who had actually met my birth father in the flesh, even more proof that I did have an American for my father.

"I sat in the Doctor's with your mum, waiting to have her pregnancy confirmed. Her husband had been serving abroad for over two years. Sure, your half American, just like my Gary!"

I wanted to squeal, and my hands gripped the wheel tighter. I knew that I was smiling in the darkness, I felt so happy at that moment, I couldn't believe what I was hearing!

I felt an overwhelming warmth for my aunt June. We were alike in some ways, we both have a strong sense of fairness for what is right, what is just. It was right that I should know about my own life, and my aunt June sensed that fairness too. I saw June with a pioneering spirit, venturing onto American soil after the war, with her baby son Gary held tightly in her arms. This took a lot of bravery, and I felt that I too had that same strength, to step out into the unknown and take a few risks. I thanked her, knowing that it must have taken a lot of courage for her to tell me. I knew that she loved my mum, her sister, very much. Yet she told me the truth.

For a brief moment there was a stunned silence in the car, when I turned and spoke again.

"June, I only know my father's name as Larry, do you remember his surname or where he came from at all?"

I held my breath, praying that she would know.

My heart sank, as she said,

"I can't remember that, jeez, that was forty years ago, I was only twenty myself!" The twang of her American accent was really noticable.

She then went on, "I can remember that he came from Kansas." My heart went in my mouth!

"Well, I'm sure that he said Kansas. I can remember Larry always looking smart. He was always at the ironing board, ironing his trousers. I think that he said that he used to work in a dry cleaner's once, but I'm not sure." We both laughed.

Suddenly my eyes misted over. I was feeling so happy, the happiest for a very long time. I gave a quick glance across to my other aunt, who had remained so silent, and so loyal, throughout our conversation. I sensed that she wanted to go. It was late and I felt drained, so I thought that we had better say goodbye now.

Just as my aunt was clambering out of the car she turned round and said, "You know Norma, I still have my Carl's old War time diary. It has lots of old War time buddies names and addresses in it, would that be any good to you?"

I felt stunned, that would be brilliant! An address book! Eagerly I agreed, and thought this must be the key to unlock the door to my past. I smiled at my aunt.

"As soon as I get back to the States, I'll send it to you." She smiled back at me, then turned and entered the house.

I switched on the ignition key, and listened to the familiar hum of the engine. A war time diary, how interesting. Larry was Carl's buddie, he had to be in that address book, surely? Excitement rose in me as I drove home. I was really on my way to finding my father now. Once I had that book clasped firmly in my hands, there would be no stopping me!

That night I felt really hopeful for the first time. My adrenalin was running high!

CHAPTER 4

A few weeks after my aunt's exciting visit to England, I came downstairs and noticed a small brown paper package lying on the front door mat. My stomach turned over, could this be my uncle Carl's war time diary that June had promised to send me? I bent down quickly and picked it up. I ripped the package open and very soon I was holding a dark green canvas book, that was obviously very old. I ran my hands all over it and then hugged it close. Again I felt a warmth towards my aunt June, for remembering to send it. I sniffed at the diary and could smell it's mustyness, the history it held oozed from it. I sat down and flicked hastily through its pages. My father had to be in this book, I muttered to myself.

On first glance at the war time diary I noticed how much the U.S. military had looked after their men. All the men's needs seemed to have been thought of. I could see that most comforts had been prepared for the G.I. soldiers, separated from their loved ones and thousands of miles from home.

I thought about the time when these intimate diaries were handed out. Maybe they wondered that some of these men would not survive, would not return home alive. Perhaps there were thoughts that they might return home alive, but not all in one piece, mentally or physically or both.

I felt an urgency to find the address section frantically turning the pages. Once found, my eyes scanned the scrawled names and addresses of these war time buddies. I felt sad as I thought that some, or maybe all of these men, might be dead. I looked and looked for Larry, but was disappointed not to find it there. With a sigh I placed the diary on a shelf, and promised myself that I'd go through it more thoroughly that evening, as I hurried off to work.

Again that night and for about the next two weeks, I studied it. The first few pages were filled with the names and addresses. I began to visualise the book being passed around at mess times or bedtimes. The young strong men, lying under canvas, on damp camp beds. The fear that these men must have felt, wondering just what was going to happen to them. These brave men, with the scent of oncoming danger in the air, prepared to give up their lives for their country, and many did.

I imagined them writing in my uncle Carl's diary. Perhaps they arranged to meet again, when the bloody war was over, but never did.

I ran my fingers over the scrawled writing, at the same time edging towards the light as I tried to decipher the correct spellings. How would these men be now? Men no longer in their prime. As I tenderly held the book, a wave of sadness came over me.

I turned the pages further on and noticed that Carl had written about his feelings on that day in May 1944, over forty years ago. I felt like an intruder as I read his private thoughts, so poignantly written.

I began after that to really concentrate on the address section of the diary. No matter how much I scanned it, I couldn't see anything like a Larry, or a Lawrence. I was beginning to feel really depressed. I had pinned all my hopes on this diary, and it didn't look like I was going to have much luck with it.

I felt myself panicking, it had to be here. After all they were buddies. I had noticed an L. Ricard there, and my eyes kept returning to it. Well, it was the only name with the initial 'L', it had to be the one. I sat and thought deeply about the name Ricard. it sounded Italian to me and I didn't look or feel anything like an Italian. I decided that I would ask Pamela Winfield, of T.R.A.C.E. what she thought about it? I photocopied the page and sent it to her. Shortly after, Pamela telephoned and after much discussion, we came to a joint conclusion that it was a possibility, and in my desperation, I decided to go for it!

Once more I picked up my writing pad and pen, and read aloud to myself, now I had the eighth Army/Airforce, Stansted airport, Essex. My aunt June had said Kansas, and now I had the name of Ricard. I let out a breath, I would go for it!

As soon as possible, I sent off for a form from the National Personell Records Centre, St. Louis, Missouri, U.S.A. (N.P.R.C.) Two weeks later the form dropped onto the mat. I sat down at the table, spreading the form out in front of me. From the first glance, I could see that there were questions that I would have to look at very carefully. When it came to filling in the surname, doubts crept into my mind, but again, I pushed them away and hurriedly finished filling it in, and went immediately to post it.

It was about three weeks later when I received a reply. I opened the envelope and took out what seemed to be a standard form. The form stated that they were unable to trace a Larry Ricard, as all the records had been destroyed in a fire at St. Louis, Missouri, in 1973.

"Oh, no!" I said out loud. I felt devastated! I sat down, filled with disbelief. Does this mean that I had absolutely no chance of finding my father now? Then as I sat there, doubts crept into my mind. Maybe this was something that the Military said to everyone, in order to protect their Veterans. I looked again at the sentence, 'a fire in 1973'. That's a likely story I thought.

Sometime later I was to learn from a 'helper' of TRACE that he actually witnessed that fire in 1973! On finding this out, I said my silent apologies to the NPRC.

It was now March 1988, and it was coming up to my daughter Hayley's birthday. To our great excitement, mum had decided to come and visit us for a few days. I had mixed feelings about this. Part of me felt apprehensive, but we had always loved each other's company, and so I looked forward to her arrival.

For some time I had been thinking about my father's surname being Ricard. It was just niggling away at me, and I couldn't get it out of my mind. I had always had a keen instinct, and I didn't feel happy about this. Mum was on her way, and deep inside I knew that I was going to have to approach her once more. My mother was the only one who would know my father's surname. What if something happened to her? What if, God forbid, she died? I couldn't bear the thought of anything happening to her, and quickly put it out of my mind! How would I bring up the subject again? Last time I approached her she firmly denied it! She hadn't even admitted to me that Larry was my father, let alone tell me his surname.

In a few short hours she would be here, she was only coming for a few days, I had to ask her. With strange feelings of impending doom hanging over me, I knew that I would have to ask her again, no matter what.

Why did I feel such an urgency. My mother had always been such a vibrant woman, so full of life.

Nothing was going to happen to her, yet I felt as if time was running out. I thought about my mother, and how she would feel about lying to me all my life! I knew my mother well enough to know that it would have over-shadowed her every waking hour. Basically, my mother was a very honest woman. I knew that she loved me and through all the traumas that I had with her husband, her love had sustained me, allowing me to keep my sanity.

Sometimes I felt so angry with her for not telling me the truth. I had gone over it and over it, trying to fathom out why. I do know that had I known at a young age, I would have gone looking for Larry. She would have known me well enough to know that I would have gone searching for my father. My mother had lost one child through death, maybe she was afraid that she would lose the other one to America? This was a strong possibility.

At last mum arrived to whoops of joy from the children. Time and again during her stay the words formed in my mind, but I feared upsetting her again. What could I do? Again I started to panic inside! I wouldn't be seeing mum for months now, I wanted to get on with my search. Again this strong feeling of time running out wafted over me. Maybe it was my father for whom time was running out, I thought?

I watched as mum loaded her luggage onto the back of her old green car. I glanced across at my children, and felt a pang. She lived so far away from us. Little did I know then that this would be the last time that she would be coming to visit us. The last time that we would walk the dog together in the park. The last time that she would play on her hands and knees with the children squealing with delight!

I was still trying to find a way to ask her. Suddenly it came to me! I was going to give her some petrol money in an envelope, why don't I put a letter in with it? I asked myself. I rushed indoors and hurriedly wrote a note. My stomach was in knots, but doing this quickly didn't give me much time to think about it. I sealed the money and the note together in an envelope and hurried back outside. Mum was already waiting in her car, and I lent through the open window and handed her the envelope.

"Mum here's some petrol money for you. Please don't open this until you get home." As I said that last sentence, I knew that it would tempt her and I immediately wished that I hadn't said that.

I felt really edgy as I saw a puzzled look pass fleetingly across her face. I was so worried about her reaction, I didn't want her to have an accident on the way home. I also feared another denial. I knew that I had to hear it from her lips this time, yet I feared another angry confrontation. I was feeling extremely guilty, for some reason. I felt as if this were all my fault! My being born was my fault that their marriage was so unhappy. I had carried their guilt firmly on my shoulders all my life!

Now mum was looking back at me from the car window. She gave a hesitant smile, and then turning to the children, she raised her hand and blew them a kiss and drove off.

All the time she was driving home, I felt on edge. I tried to immerse myself in the house and so when the telephone rang, I never thought that it would be my mother, as not enough time had elapsed for her to arrive home. I jumped as I heard her voice on the other end! I took a deep breath, bracing myself for another bout of her anger, but instead she sounded very different.

"Norma, I've just stopped at the service station for a cup of coffee and I've read your note." My heart went into my mouth, and I was aware that the palms of my hands were sweating as I gripped the phone.

"Norma, why didn't you talk to me about this while I was at your house?" She seemed very calm.

"I was afraid that you would be really angry with me again!" I felt like a naughty little girl, back in my childhood.

"Look, we can't talk here, but we must talk about this. I'll go home now. I've got about another two hours' drive, as soon as I get home, and if he's gone out with the dog, I'll phone you." Her voice sounded so relieved, more like her normal self. I took a deep breath, and slowly exhaled. As I replaced the receiver I knew that the next few hours were going to seem endless.

Questions were going round and round in my mind? What on earth was she going to tell me? Would she tell me anything at all? I prayed that there would be no more lies, please, no more lies, I said silently to myself.

I knew that whatever happened I had to get Larry's surname out of her, no matter what. That was the most important thing! I was feeling sufficiently strong enough now to be firm with her. I would demand it, if I had to. Please don't let me get angry with her, I thought. After all, she had been through it during the war, I still felt for her, for the position she found herself in. Then a few years after the war, her first born child had died! I decided then that I would not reproach her verbally, no matter what happened.

The phone was ringing, I ran out into the hall and lunged at the receiver.

"Hello, mum, are you alright?" I said breathlessly.

In a quiet voice, she replied, "He's just gone out with the dog."

My heart was pounding as I blurted out, "Mum, please tell me the truth about Larry," I pleaded in a very calm subdued voice.

She said, "Yes, he is your father."

I felt the breath go out of me! There was a part of me that felt she would never admit it, ever! Now, at last this forty year old secret was out!

"Tell me about him, mum." I was silently praying that she wouldn't change her mind.

"Well, I told you about him when you were a child. I met him through June's Carl. They were both stationed at Stansted. You have your American grandmother's name of Jean." I felt a pang. I had been walking around with my American grandmother's name of Jean all my life, and I hadn't known it. How sad, I thought.

"You are a lot like me, but you are like him too. You have his eyes." I felt myself go warm at that, I somehow knew that I would have his eyes.

She went on speaking, seeming to unburden herself of a really heavy load.

"He was a very kind man, Norma, you take after him in that way." Tears filled my eyes.

My mother was talking about my father. I couldn't quite take in the conversation, a conversation that I had dreamed of having for such a long time. Now it was actually happening, there were no more false statements, no barriers between us anymore.

My mother continued to talk, "I wrote to Larry telling him that I thought I was pregnant, but I never heard from him again," she said sadly.

"I used to write to his mother and she told me that after he got back from the war, he went to stay with her."

My mouth dropped open and for a few seconds I couldn't speak! I really was half-American! The man that I had always called 'dad' was definitely not my father. Until my mother had actually confirmed this to me, there was always this little minute piece of doubt niggling away at the back of my mind. I sighed, now I knew it was really true!

Suddenly in a rush, I thought, I really could have a biological father somewhere. There was chance that he could still be alive. I might look just like him, after all mum says I have his eyes.

"There was an American Indian in the family." She quickly spoke again, almost I felt, unburdening herself of this dark secret. A secret that had been hidden deep in the recess of her mind, for so many years.

"An American Indian!" I gasped! "That's amazing!" I had always had an empathy with the Indians while watching 'Cowboys and Indians' on the T.V. as a child. Now I know why! They are in my blood! My mind was racing along. I had so much that I wanted to ask her, I didn't want to have any regrets after I had put the phone down. What if I never got the chance to speak to her again about this, she lived so far away. I knew that I was reeling from our conversation, but I had to keep myself calm.

"Mum can you remember where he came from at all?"

I held my breath!

"NO!" She replied firmly!

My heart sank. Somehow I couldn't quite believe that she couldn't remember where he came from, after all she had written to his mother, how can someone forget where that was? I knew that she was still lying.

I began to gently question her more. "Did he have any children, mum?" I hoped desperately that she would say yes.

"Yes, three."

I felt excitement rising in me.

"Do you know if they were boys or girls?"

"I don't know." She sounded exasperated.

Suddenly she said, "He went back to the States in March 1946."

My mouth dropped open again. She was actually volunteering information to me. I couldn't believe what I was hearing! Then a deep sadness wafted over me, as I said, "Mum, I think it would have been better if you'd had me adopted. It would have been far better for me, and it would have been better for you and him."

Her voice rose higher. "What, give you up! You were mine. I loved you. I wanted you! I could never have given you up!"

I felt myself go warm at her words. She couldn't have said a nicer thing to me. I will remember her voice saying those words, forever!

Suddenly I remembered the most important thing, "Mum, I need to know Larry's surname."

"Oh, I'll tell you that the next time I see you. You know when the military found out about our liason, they sent him back as quickly as they could!" I sensed that she was hedging about the surname. To this day I don't know if all that she told me was the truth.

"Mum!" I pleaded.

"Please tell me Larry's surname?"

"Oh, I'll tell you the next time I see you. You know he was a really nice man, you don't have any worries about that. I can still see him now, walking away from me, up the garden path, with his head in his hands, crying!" She suddenly sobbed into the phone, as her voice broke. A lump came into my throat and tears trickled silently down my face. I still felt an urgency, through my tears, to get my father's surname whatever happened. I had to get it before she put the telephone down. I was feeling decidely edgy by now.

"Mum, I need to know my father's name," I said, almost through gritted teeth!

"Why, you're not going to search for him, are you?"

"Yes!"

I heard something bordering on hysteria in my own voice as I said, "Mum, I can't wait to see you again. I might not see you again for months!" I could feel myself beginning to panic! I wasn't going to get it!

"Oh, you'll cause such trouble if you try to trace him!" She sounded resolute.

I thought, this is not fair! It is just not fair! This was my life, and it was my father!

"Mum, please tell me his surname!"

"Well...."

"Look, it's my right to know my father's name!" I said, lowering my voice.

All of a sudden the tension seemed to ebb away from the conversation, it seemed as if she had finally given in, when she said,

Yes, it is your right to know, it's McCloud, M c C L O U D." She spelt it out.

I felt stunned. I felt rivetted to the spot! She had told me at last and she had actually spelt it out! As I was still reeling from her words, she spoke softly, "His full name was Lawrence McCloud."

Now excitement bubbled up in my throat, for a few seconds I was speechless! She's told me his name and it was Lawrence after all! She's even spelt his name to me, then a fearful thought came over me. What made her spell it? I hadn't asked her. Oh, God, I hope that she hasn't spelt it incorrectly to throw me off the track! Surely she wouldn't do that to me? Throughout my search, I always had a nagging doubt about the spelling of McCloud.

73

"You know, Norma, I would have told you before I died. I had made up my mind about that a long time ago," she said sadly.

I was unable to answer as a lump came to my throat, and I felt enormous gratitude towards my mother, for although she had lied to me all my life, it must have taken great strength to tell me at last!

At last our phone conversation was ending, and I fumbled for a tissue to wipe my eyes. My mother had lived with this lie for over forty years, and now at last she was able to let go of this 'skeleton' in her cupboard. I had such mixed feelings at that time. I felt sad for her husband and the child they had lost, yet at the same time I felt deliriously happy that I finally knew the name of my own father.

I wondered again whether my biological father was still alive. This dark family secret had finally been exorcised. Now, would I finally get to meet him?

I wanted to scream! I would find this Lawrence McCloud. I would leave no stone unturned until I stood face to face with him, whether he liked it or not!

CHAPTER 5

It was now evening. My children were asleep, and I sat in a daze, thinking about the phone call that I had had with my mother earlier in the day. Our conversation went round and round in my head, like a long playing record.

I thought about my father's surname. It sounded Scottish to me. I remembered reading somewhere that the American Indians would put the 'Mc' in front of their names to make them sound more western, maybe a hundred years ago my ancestors were called 'Cloud'. The thought of that was fascinating!

All of a sudden it came to me that the name of Ricard, was no longer relevant! Thank God, I found out from mum when I did. I broke out in a sweat when I realised that I could have spent weeks, months or even years before I found out the truth. Maybe I would never have found out. I quickly swept those thoughts away, now it was time for me to look forward, no more looking back! I had to press on, enthusiasm was pulsing through my veins!

I seemed to have renewed energy, I felt so much stronger. I knew that there was a good chance of finding my father now that I had his real name.

The next day I lifted out the grey box that I kept my 'search' papers in, and began rummaging through for the address of a geneology directory in the U.S.A. I finally found it and hurriedly filled in the order form and sent it off. Two weeks later

I was in possession of three thousand four hundred and twenty seven people with the surname of McCloud. As I began to flick through the pages, hopelessness swept over me. If my father were here, I had about as much chance of finding him, as twirling a pin around and sticking it in the pages!

I took stock of my situation and decided to get organised. My search, I said to myself, was quite simply a process of elimination. Right, my father probably still lives in Kansas, or at least his family does. I picked up the McCloud directory once more, and flicked through it again until I found the section that covered Kansas. I let my eyes travel very slowly down the page, looking for anyone with the initial 'L'. I stopped suddenly, I could only see one, but there was a Norma J. I thought that was rather uncanny, and maybe an omen. I decided then that she would be the first person I would write to. Sadly I never received a reply.

The enormity of the task that lay ahead of me was daunting. I felt like a climber must feel, looking up, craning my neck to see the top of the mountain, the mountain that I knew I was going to have to climb, if I was ever going to know inner peace.

All my life I'd loved a challenge. I knew that deep down, I would never let this one beat me!

I began to write to my McCloud directory. I knew that I would have to be super sensitive, and so I wrote at first that I was looking for an old family 'friend'. I always enclosed a self-addressed envelope, and an international reply coupon. If we need our allies help, then we should not expect them to put their hands in their pockets as well, I reasoned. Sadly, when I wrote to people out of the directory, I usually never received a reply. There was one very kind man, Leason McCloud, he photocopied his whole family tree for me, and commented that there was no 'Lawrence' in it. I knew that Americans are on the whole mistrustful of people, and don't like strange letters from strange people, landing on their doorstep, and I could understand that.

Whenever I got 'stuck' over the years, I would turn to my McCloud directory and write a few more letters, at least I felt as if I was doing something!

During the years of my search, I had tended to keep my search for my father to myself. Occasionally I would mention something to my friends, but generally I quietly ferreted away, something like a mole, silently going through a long dark tunnel, with the hope of eventually reaching the light!

I felt a special bond with other G.I. 'babies'. After all, they understood my need to see my father's face, that inner drive, which is so hard to explain to others who already know their 'genetic make-up'.

So with great tenacity, I continued my letter writing. After about two years of writing letters in the theme of looking for a 'family friend', I met the father of Veronica, (another G.I. baby). He was in England for a visit with his 'new found' daughter. For a time we chatted together about my own search and he said, "Look, I wouldn't feel very happy about someone writing to me from England, and not telling me the truth." He looked at me and smiled.

I nodded my head in agreement.

"We Americans are suspicious of everyone. It's far better if you are honest and just write that you are searching for your father."

The more I thought about what he said, the more it made sense to me. I know that generally the British are far more sensitive about people's feelings, especially in circumstances like mine. I would not like to upset my father or his family, but I did feel that honesty was the best policy. I decided that from then on I would always tell my story with sensitivity, but with honesty as well. Time was running out and 'hedging' around the real story was just wasting time. My letters began with an apology, 'if I have the wrong man, do you know anyone with the same name of Lawrence McCloud?'

About the same time that I received my McCloud directory, I wrote to the National Army Museum, in London. I had no idea how on earth they could help me, except that they might have some lists of the American soldiers who served here in World War Two. But they quickly wrote back that they were unable to help me.

I had also come across the American Airforce situated in Texas. I wrote a letter of enquiry to them and received a form from them to fill in. At first I felt quite excited and thought they must think that there's a chance. I sat down with a cup of tea and began to read the questions on the form. It requested full name, rank, social security number, and date of birth. I sat back in my chair and let out a howl! Was this letter some kind of joke? I had explained to them my situation. If I had all this information I wouldn't need to write to them, would I? I wondered if this base had actual fisches, lists of men who had served in England in the second World War, or obviously they must have misunderstood my request?

My mountain seemed insurmountable!

In June 1988, I was sent the name and address of a Virgil Thompson, who lived in Lima, Ohio, U.S.A. I felt excited when I got a new 'helper' always feeling that maybe this person will find my father for me. After a short time, Virgil replied. I laughed as I looked at the miniscule piece of paper that Virgil had written on. I peered closely at the miniscule writing that matched the paper. There was the name of a Lawrence McCloud, and this man's address was in Kansas! I was shocked!

It seemed to fit. I stared at the address in disbelief.

I read it again and again. It was the right name and it was the right State. Could it possibly be that easy? I was beginning to feel very excited, but a part of me was suppressing this, yet I rushed to the phone dialling Pamela Winfield's number as quickly as I could. We spoke and she suggested I try International Directory enquiries. Maybe this man could be reached on the phone.

My stomach turned over. My father could be only a telephone call away! At the same time, Pamela gave me the name of Harold Ludwig, who was a 'helper' of TRACE, and lived in St. Louis, Missouri.

"He'll make a telephone call for you," Pamela commented.

With great excitement, I managed to get a telephone for this Lawrence McCloud in Kansas. I had rung Directory Enquiries, and then suddenly the operator was giving me this man's number. I replaced the receiver and stared at the phone. This could be my father. I tried to muster up the courage to telephone him, but was just not brave enough. Questions went round in my mind. What if his wife answered it, what would I say to her? What if this Mr McCloud slammed the phone down on me? What a shock he would have on hearing an English accent at the other end of the line. Underneath it all was this terrible fear of rejection. If I found my father and then he rejected me, it might be just too much for me to bear.

I decided that I would write to this Harold Ludwig and ask if he would be so kind as to phone for me. I decided that at the same time I wrote to Harold, I would also write to this Mr McCloud in Kansas.

Two weeks later I picked up a letter from the mat, and daring to look, I noticed that it was from the McClouds. I ripped the letter open, my heart in my mouth. Was this letter from my father? My heart sank! It was from Mr McCloud's wife, writing to say that they didn't know of the man I was asking about, and did I know that there are many ways to spell McCloud? I noticed that at the very bottom of her letter, she had written some of the various ways. Mcloud, Mccleud, Macloud. I knew that she was right, and the idea of it was to plague me all through my search, even until the end.

I read and re-read Mrs McCloud's letter. Why had she written and not her husband? I was beginning to feel suspicious of it. Someone had told me once that American wives, as a rule, opened all the mail, including their husband's. Maybe Mr McCloud had not even seen my letter. How would I ever know?

Once I had found out about my birth, I had heard other stories of rejection from some G.I. fathers. I knew that some of these fathers would not, or will not, own up to their indiscretions. They will not admit to anything. They had their reasons. Perhaps it was the fear of disrupting their family, or understandably, worried that these war-babies were after their money? Again I felt for the American wives, but then I would ask myself, what about us? We are the children of these liaisons, don't we have any say in this? After all, I believe that we war-babes have paid for the 'sins' of our fathers and our mothers!

It was July 1988, when I first wrote to the Veterans Affairs, (VA) in Jefferson City, Missouri. It's there to help ex-service men and women who might need help in anyway, maybe with their pension or rather sadly, with a funeral.

I wrote to them, enquiring about my father. They replied that they were bound by the Official Secrets Act and any information that they had was in the strictest confidence. They were sorry, but they could not assist me in my search. I felt really despondent, and warned myself that I was going to have to get used to these kinds of answers!

Would no one help a daughter find a father, before it was too late? I pleaded silently.

In the back of my mind was the puzzling aspect of the man in Kansas. I would go over it and over it. Suddenly, I thought, why don't I write to a social worker? Most big towns in the States had a Town Hall, so I decided to write to a social worker at the Town Hall in Kansas City.

In a short while, I had received a very nice, friendly reply from a Julia Hall. It seemed a little strange as it was a handwritten letter, and it was in an ordinary envelope.

Julia had written that she was a case worker for the welfare department, and served the 'poor and indigent'. She continued that she had checked the records and there was no Lawrence McCloud claiming assistance. Julia went on to list ways in which I might find my father and I felt my spirits soar, with her last sentence, 'I will try to help you.'

I quickly wrote back to her. A social worker was going to help me. It was wonderful, I couldn't believe how lucky I was. I waited and waited for a reply from her. After some time, I received a very official looking letter, informing me that there was no such person as a Julia Hall working for them, and they were unable to assist me further. Deflated, I slumped down in my chair. How could this be? This letter was extremely puzzling. Maybe Julia was going to try to help me in a private capacity, but someone had intervened? I felt as if I was going slightly mad! It is a mystery that will never be solved.

The wind had been well and truly 'knocked out of my sails,' but I soon picked myself up, determined to carry on with my quest!

CHAPTER 6

It was now the summer of 1988, the time of the year that we made our annual visit to Dorset to see mum and 'dad'. I was blissfully unaware of the trauma that the next few weeks were going to bring me.

Our arrival coincided with the annual carnival. The weather was sunny and very warm and mum was at the Intercity train to greet myself and the children. We were always pleased to see each other, and after hugs and kisses we made our way to her neat home. The beds had been made up in the spare room, so we hurriedly deposited our suitcases in there, and with great excitement started to make our way down the steep hill and into the quaint town, where the carnival was about to start. We had spoken very briefly to 'dad' and I always sensed his unease at our being there. He had always been very possessive with mum, but now I knew why.

We were on our way to the carnival, with only happy thoughts in my mind. Suddenly I glanced across at my mother, and a feeling of unease came over me as I looked at her. I noticed fleetingly that she looked preoccupied and very tired. Her boundless energy seemed to be replaced by a kind of lethargy. Frowning with concern, I linked my arm in hers, subconsciously aiding her down the hill. As we watched the carnival, we lost mum in the crowds, eventually meeting up with her later. I braced myself for her displeasure at that happening, but it never surfaced, almost as if she hadn't the spirit anymore.

Gradually as the days passed by, her lethargy became even more apparent to me. I tried to convince myself that it was just her age, after all she wasn't getting any younger.

The day before our holiday was to end, I sat beside her in her old green car. The car seemed to have sprouted wings, it was flying along at quite a speed. I felt apprehensive, this isn't like mum, I thought. The lush green gorse rushed by and as I gazed out of the window, suddenly mum's voice broke my reverie.

"You know, Norma, he has never forgiven me, for having you!" She kept her eyes straight ahead.

I turned around to look at her.

"He has always wanted to punish me somehow."

Just as I opened my mouth to reply, there was a commotion from my two children in the back of the car. I turned away from her and the moment of unity between us was lost forever. She was never to speak to me again on the subject, as dreadful events were to overtake our lives and things were never to be the same again.

Three weeks later, mum started to be dreadfully sick. She was admitted immediately to hospital. I travelled to Dorset filled with dread. Was this the impending doom that I sensed sometime before? As soon as I saw her I knew that there was something dreadfully wrong. I felt powerless to help her. I went into total shock when told that she had a brain tumour!

Eight weeks later my mother died.

I moved around in a fog! The shock was unbelievable! I felt as if my right arm had been wrenched from its socket. She was only sixty-three, I cried. It wasn't fair! Her loss was so painful, too much at times for me to bear. I cried until there were no more tears, I couldn't imagine our lives without her. At times I was so angry at her for leaving us. Why didn't she get help sooner, I sobbed.

'Dad' was distraught! I knew that his conscience was pricking him. "I hope that I didn't make your mother sick," he said.

He leant on me and in my shock and compassion, I allowed him to. I remembered my mother's words shortly before she died, "He'll have another woman, before you can turn around!"

How well she knew him, for on the very day that we placed my mother's ashes in the ground, I watched, stunned, as he ran frantically up and down streets, knocking on stranger's doors, searching for an old lady friend!

After my mother's death, my step-father was lost.

He visited us a few times, something he had never done, actually coming to our house for the first time, because of my mother's funeral. Although she had died in Dorset, she had been born and bred in Enfield. My sister, Linda, her daughter who died, was buried in Enfield, it seemed right that my mother's ashes be interred with Linda. Mother and daughter reunited, the thought of that helped ease the pain of my grief.

Once 'dad' had located his long-lost lady friend, he returned to his old ways, and we were forgotten once more. All the time 'dad' was unaware that I knew he was not my biological father. It was several years later that this lie was laid to rest, resulting in a final severing of the ties that had bound us together.

After my mother's death, I had this sense of loss, and a terrible emptiness. I felt like an orphan, then one day I realised that I might not be an orphan. I might have a natural father still alive somewhere. Maybe this man might not want to know me, but if I was able to find him, not meeting me would be his loss, I told myself.

It was November 1988. Mum had been dead two months and I had known about my father for two years. I tried to get myself motivated again, but I seemed to be doing things like a robot. I felt so afraid to leave the house for some reason. Life could not touch me if I stayed indoors. I realise now, that it was a classic case of bereavement, which slowly with time, faded away. I believe that I will never get over my mother's death, but I have now 'come to terms' with it.

The sun shone through the windows as I sifted through the day's mail. I smiled as I realised that one of the letters was from Harold Ludwig, my 'helper' from Missouri. As I began to read his letter, I felt quite excited. He wrote that he had actually telephoned the Lawrence McCloud in Kansas. My heart went in my mouth and I quickly sat down. He said that Mr McCloud's wife had answered the phone, and appeared very pleasant. She explained to Harold that her husband had been in the Korean war and not the second World War. I felt immediately suspicious. Why hadn't her husband spoken to Harold? He hadn't answered my letter. This man could be the one, how would we ever get to know? I tried to think of a plan. In the end I decided to write to him again, only this time I'd enclose a photograph of myself. I heard that sending a photo just nudged the father into claiming his child.

As well as phoning those McClouds in Kansas, Harold had taken to phoning all the McClouds he could find in the Kansas area. He was as determined as I was in ferreting this man out! Later he sent me a copy of the list, with the comments he'd made beside each 'McCloud'. I felt a pang and was so grateful to Harold and all that he was doing to help me.

Harold wrote again. He had phoned the McClouds in Kansas a second time, and he was now having grave doubts about the authenticity of these people. So Harold was thinking along the same lines as I was? Harold questioned this man's age. Was he really young enough to have been in the Korean war? I wondered that as well, and waited with anticipation for a reply to my letter that I sent to those McClouds.

I was very relieved as 1988 went out and the new year came in! I never wanted to spend another year like it again! I felt as if I'd aged about ten years. Although I was mentally and physically drained, I was feeling very philosophical about my mother's death. A few years before I had an 'out of body' experience, and this experience changed my life. It changed my whole outlook on death, that there is no death, and I believe that our body is just a 'shell', a 'heavy overcoat' we carry around until we pass over ourselves. Since her death I had felt my mother's presence all around me. I know that death is a part of life, and life is very good. Life must go on. I said to myself. I had to be strong for my children, who had been through the sadness as well. We decided that a trip to Disney World in Florida, would do us all the world of good. I set about organising it: planning this and immersing myself in my search would keep my mind off things and keep me going.

During this time I had been given the name of a man called Leroy Stover. He lived in Ohio U.S.A. and was a researcher for the Eighth Army/Airforce. For a very short time I was once more getting excited at a new lead, especially as Leroy had been at Stansted, Essex, England, at the same time as I believed that my father was. I wrote a hurried letter, but was soon knocked back by his comments when he replied.

'That although he had been at Stansted, his unit had left for France, so he was unable to help me.' He added at the end, 'I will try to help you in any other way.'

At that time, anyone's offer of help was very gratefully received by me. At times I felt so humble, that people should want to help me, even though we had never met.

Each morning as I came downstairs, my eyes would be drawn

like a magnet to the front doormat. At times my emotions were haywire. I felt that I just couldn't carry on with this incessant searching, it was taking over my life. Then after two weeks of feeling so down, I would start to feel all fired up and ready to start again. I would find my father! It was my right to find him.

Always lurking in the back of my mind, were these McClouds in Kansas. Until I had completely eliminated them, how on earth could I move on?

It was April 1989. The phone was ringing, I put down my wash cloth and hurried to the telephone.

"Hi, Norma Jean?" An American accent, I thought?

"Yes" I answered, puzzled.

"Well, this is Harold Ludwig, and I'm here in London for a visit." I gasped! "I'm phoning to see if we could meet up sometime?"

It was finally arranged that we would come to his Hotel the following Sunday. As I replaced the phone, I felt so excited. How my life is changing, I said to myself. I knew that I was gaining in confidence all the time. I looked forward to meeting Harold and his family, and to actually talk with Harold face to face about my search would be wonderful.

I was feeling decidely nervous as I arrived with my husband and two children at the Hotel where Harold was staying. This was my first meeting with my 'helper' and yet somehow I knew that we would 'get along!'

Before long we fell into an easy banter, as if we had known each other for years!

As we sat facing each other, we began to speak in depth about my search, especially those McClouds in Kansas. Eventually we came to the mutual conclusion that Harold would make one more tentative phone call to them, and try to glean something more from the conversation.

Later that day, we all went on a trip around Westminster Abbey, posing for photographs along the way. These I will always treasure as memories of a lovely day.

Harold had been a G.I. soldier stationed at Stoke-on-Trent, England, during the second World War. Many years later he returned to British soil in search of an old girlfriend he once knew. He posted a notice on a bulletin board and this gesture was published in a national newspaper. Pamela Winfield spotted this advert, and being a shrewd lady, decided to barter with Harold.

"If I help you in your search, Harold, will you help G.I. babes in theirs?" she laughed.

It was an offer he couldn't refuse, and so Harold was enlisted as an indefatigable 'helper' of T.R.A.C.E. Sadly, Harold never did find that old lady friend.

A few weeks after Harold's visit, we began to prepare for our visit to Disney World, Florida. I had also arranged that we would pay a visit to my aunt June, who lived near Panama City, Florida. I began to feel really excited and yet I still found it hard to come to terms with the fact that I was half-American. I had heard that I would be entitled to actually be an American citizen by my birth. First I had to find my father.

The time came for our holiday, and as we boarded the plane, a feeling of unreality swept over me. I was going to America where my father lives, or did live. I wanted to shout it to everyone as soon as I boarded the plane! I leaned across my son, and peered out of the aircraft window. Was that really America below us? This was actually America, a country that was a real part of me, and yet I had never known it. I felt a sadness for all the years of not knowing that I had this heritage. I was a part of the first Americans, the American Indians. I wondered as I flew over the land, just who the American Indian was, and from what tribe had they come? I was flooded at that point with a determination to find out one day! A part of me was angry. I should be getting off this plane with an American passport clasped firmly in my hand!

The warm climate, and the childish experiences were all that we needed. It lifted us, and somehow I now knew that travelling was in my blood. I felt like I wanted to see the world.

After a week in Disney World, we boarded a Greyhound Bus and travelled four hundred miles to Youngstown, Florida, where my aunt June the G.I. bride lived. We were to experience with her an 'outback' holiday, the real Florida.

Since the visit that June made to England, when she helped me so much, I felt eternally grateful to her. As we travelled on the Greyhound Bus, I began to think about June, and what she must have experienced as a young bride. How frightened she must have felt, not knowing exactly where she was going, her baby son, Gary clasped tightly in her arms. She must have worried about the kind of life she was going to have, and been desolate to leave her loving family behind. She had told me that when she first arrived, Carl had taken her to live with his parents in Indiana. (Where in 1947, she gave birth to a daughter, Judy.) On her arrival in Indiana she had been so shocked to see an old wooden shack, and the toilet just a hole dug into the ground. She had felt so alone, she said. It had been very hard in England, with the rationing, but it was nothing to the deprivation she experienced there! She had been so homesick and desperate to return to England, but there had been no hope of that, they were so poor. She had realised too late, that she was a prisoner of her own making.

Finally the Greyhound Bus pulled into the station at Youngstown, Panama City. It all felt very strange, but it was lovely to see my aunt once more. We found the surroundings vastly different to the luxury hotel from which we had just left. Her home was a mobile type vehicle situated on an acre of grass, and at the very bottom of her garden were the Everglades.

"There are alligators in there!" warned my aunt.

Around the side of her place were rabbit hutches, standing high off the ground. The rabbits were white albino ones and the children squealed as they gently poked their fingers through the wire mesh cages, trying to stroke them.

"These rabbits belong to my renter," my aunt explained. "He keeps them for eating."

The children gasped, and looked at her with disbelief. Feeling sorry for them we bent down and pulled at the grass, poking it through the mesh for them to eat.

"Jeez, they've never ate grass before," my aunt commented, looking surprised.

Every morning we would be awakened by ducks banging their beaks on the back door.

"Well, they are asking for bread for their breakfast," my aunt explained to the children, laughing.

June had a black cat called, appropriately, 'Blackie'. She ran so fast, if you didn't look quick enough you missed her! She also shared her home with a bright green and purple lizard, who lived in a hole in the wall. I hadn't realised that until the day before we left. My aunt had gone to work and I was hoovering, while the children played outside. Suddenly this lizard sprang out in front of me, and it was running at top speed! I think I matched its speed though, as screaming, I dived into the next room, not knowing whether to laugh or cry!

As my aunt had said, there were alligators in the river. It was a warm evening and June suggested that we take her small boat up the river for a ride. We were very excited at this prospect, and the children donned their life-jackets and clambered onto the boat. Then we were on our way. A gentle breeze was blowing as quietly we made our way up the river, passing the alien scenery. I don't know who spotted it first, but suddenly from out of the gnarled trees, an eagle swooped low down in front of our boat! Our mouths dropped open, for in its talons was a huge fish! We watched in awed silence as it flew across the river landing in a far tree.

Shortly after this had happened, we became increasingly concerned about the outboard engine on the boat. We could hear the engine struggling to keep going. Then after a lot of phut-phutting, the engine ceased! I felt panic, after all, didn't my aunt say that there were alligators in the river? I turned round to look at the children, and managed to stifle a laugh! There were the children, life jackets on huddled together like 'waifs in a storm'. After trying to fix the engine, my aunt and I decided we'd have to row. Darkness was beginning to fall, and in Florida it gets dark very quickly. An eeriness fell over the river. I felt afraid for the first time. It only needed one swift, swipe of an alligator's tail, there in the dark, and that would be the end of us!

Luckily for us, the 'calvalry' came to our rescue! Two men in a fast speed boat appeared out of the gloomy mist and towed us home.

I had thought about this time spent with my aunt, and decided that it would be a good opportunity to speak to her again about my father. It was far better for me to sit beside her to discuss this, rather than ask her in a letter. I racked my brains for anything that I could ask her, that she could possibly know. There could be the slightest thing that she might think unimportant, but in the end might lead me to Larry.

June remembered again how particular Larry had been about

his clothes. She remembered that he had smoked a pipe. I thought back to that large photo at my grandmother's, and could distinctly 'see' that he had a pipe in his left hand.

It was time to say goodbye to my aunt and our holiday of a lifetime. We were very sorry to leave, but looked forward to the future, and the prospect of finding my father sometime soon.

The weather was extremely cold as we arrived back in England. We made our way home, feeling very weary, to find a pile of letters on the front door mat. We had to push against the door to force the mail into a heap on the floor, and then we gingerly stepped over it.

Later I sorted through it, sighing, as most were only bills! But there was one in amongst the pile from Harold. My hopes rose as I opened it. Maybe he has some good news, I thought optimistically. But my hopes were dashed, as he wrote about his holiday in England. I was sadly disappointed, but I told myself, Norma, you have to persevere. No one is going to find your father for you, you've got to do this yourself! But then I thought, yes, but it is nice to have a little help from your friends!

In July Harold sent me a large brown envelope.

I opened it up, wondering what he had sent now. It was a magazine called 'How To Locate A Buddie'. I read it eagerly. From time to time, when I was feeling low, I would pick this up and look for another idea that I might try.

Harold had also enclosed a photocopy of a letter that Mrs McCloud in Kansas had sent him. The letter was very pleasant, but there were undertones of exasperation. Once more she insisted that her husband was not the man I was looking for. She reiterated that he was in the Korean War, and not World War Two. She had enclosed some copies of their local directory, which had several spellings of the name of McCloud. A strong feeling of unease came over me. What if my mother had spelt it incorrectly? After reading that letter, all my mistrust in those McClouds fell away. I knew then that they were telling the truth, after all, she wouldn't have taken the trouble to write this, would she?

I thought about all those wasted months. But then I reconciled myself to the fact that I had done other things as well. I remembered back to the time I received Mr McCloud's address in Kansas, how excited I was! I wondered, would I ever experience the real thing?

In that same big brown envelope Harold had put in a note for me, saying the same thoughts as I had, those McClouds were telling the truth.

Now I was right back where I started. I felt that I had to stop my search, at least for a while. It was just like looking for a needle in a haystack, really! I didn't want to carry on anymore. I would just have to accept my past, as it was. I could do nothing more!

A few weeks later, I suddenly felt an energy, a quiet force beginning to urge me on once more. No, I would not let this thing beat me! I must have no regrets in my life. I would have another try. I would push on! I walked over and placed the record of 'Somewhere Out There' on my music centre. I sat down and listened once more to the poignant words. At least we could be sleeping underneath the same big sky! I muttered to myself.

I began my search again, by writing to Maxwell Airforce Base, in Alabama, U.S.A. This was the Headquarters of the United States Airforce Historical Research Center. On July 11th 1989, I received their reply. In my letter of enquiry to them, I had asked for the names of the units that had been based at Stansted during the 2nd World War. They replied that it was the Tactical Air Depot, that was there at that time. I frowned, I wasn't really sure how that could help me. I knew that I was trying to take a very wide perspective of my search, and there might just be something that would turn up from somewhere that would lead me to my father.

In the meantime TRACE had given me the address of a Gayle B. Agency in the U.S.A. It was not a detective agency, more an informal tracking agency. I quickly wrote off a letter of enquiry to her, asking if she could possibly help me.

I felt quite emotional when I received her letter back. Gayle said that there was a couple of checks that she could do for fifty dollars. I felt elated! This was great! I felt more hopeful than I had done in a very long time. This was a different avenue of my search. I hurried to the bank, ordered an international cheque, and promptly sent it off. Finding the extra money was a problem, but I said to myself, what's money to life!

It was November when I received a reply. My stomach turned over as I read her letter. She had enclosed the name and address of a Lawrence McCloud living in Savannah, Georgia. I swallowed hard as I studied her letter and thought, this man seems to fit the bill, but then on second thoughts, so did that man in Kansas!

I looked at the address again. It felt really strange that this man should come from Georgia. Somehow, to me it didn't feel right. Once again questions went through my mind. What if my aunt June had the wrong State? After all, her husband must have had many buddies. Perhaps one of those others came from Georgia? It was all so long ago, people remember things differently.

I looked at the information sent to me. My eyes travelled down the paper. There was quite a bit on this man. There was his date of birth, his social security number, his dates of service were from September 1945 to February 1947. I felt elated!

These dates certainly fit with my conception, then I remembered that my aunt had said to me that it was a romance that lasted several months. if that were true, and I knew that I had been conceived in December 1945, this man couldn't have enlisted, been trained and sent overseas in such a short time, as well as conceiving me along the way! Eventually I came to the conclusion that the agency must be pretty sure about this, so I'd give it a go.

I sat down and picked up my pad and pen, and composed yet another letter. At that time I was still writing that I was looking for an 'old family friend'. I posted the letter as quickly as I could, and one to Harold, letting him know of this man in Georgia and of this new development in my search.

Harold replied, 'Sometimes the G.I. would mention to his lady friend the nearest town to where he actually lived, as it was probably easier that way.' Maybe my father did that with my mother.

He wrote, 'This guy ain't here!' (meaning Kansas)! Contained in that same letter were some really handy hints from Harold for me to take note of?

1- 'Never complain about how many times you have written.

2 - Always write your letter to the highest person you can find.

3 - Always telephone if you can, and always tell the truth.

4 - Always make sure that you include all the relevant details on the phone.

5 - Always call back, never slam the phone down!'

As if I would, I thought.

Harold then went on to ask if he could borrow Carl's address book? I felt excited at the prospect of that. Thinking that it would be good to have another pair of eyes looking at it.

His letter went on, 'You never know, you might find a father, brother, sister, aunts, uncles, life long friends.

After reading Harold's enthusiastic letter that day, I felt myself agreeing with everything that he had to say.

I felt that what he was really saying was, if you want something really bad enough, you've got to fight tooth and nail for it! That was my philosophy too.

I knew in my heart of hearts that it was fair to look for my father. It was fair and reasonable for me to want to know the family history. It was right that I should know about anything medical that might run in my biological family.

Throughout the time of my search, I would find myself talking to others about it. Sometimes I would sense a barrier of the unenlightened, and receive a comment, "I'd let sleeping dogs lie, if I were you." It would make me feel angry inside, but then my anger would turn into pity. I always felt sorry for someone who was unable to 'put themselves in someone else's position.' Usually these people with their thoughtless comments would know just what their father's face looked like, knew their father's name and whether they had their father's eyes or not.

How narrow minded some people are, I would say to myself, and feel very sorry for them.

For myself, I just happen to be one of those people with a very strong need to find out about the other half of my genetic make-up. Perhaps it was because I had grown up with a distant, shadowy figure, who was supposed to be my father, but never acted like one. Perhaps it was because I'd never had a male in my life that had truly cared about me. The lack of a father as a role model has affected my whole life. I had just begun to face it and I knew that I was beginning to change.

CHAPTER 7

After writing to Mr McCloud in Georgia, weeks passed by and I heard nothing from him. I decided to write again, only this time I enclosed a photo as well. I hadn't many photos of myself, as it always seemed to be me actually taking them!

As I folded the letter and carefully placed it with the photo in the envelope, I thought about this man, maybe my father? If I looked like him, then this photo, I reasoned, would be like a magnet pulling him across the ocean.

I wrote the same type of letter again, popped it into the post box, and began the wait once more.

I had received the winter newsletter from TRACE. I felt a pang as I looked at the list of people who had managed to trace their fathers. Admittedly some of them had not ended in happiness, but I yearned for the time when my name would eventually be there. Would that ever happen?

Time and again I had thought of all the scenerios that might face me, should I track him down. I still always came up with the same answer that I might find a happy ending. But how would I know unless I tried? I had to face the fact of rejection, but my self-worth was now rising. If my father did not want to know me, then all I wanted was a photograph and the family history, and I decided that I would get on with the rest of my life.

I had hoped that I wouldn't face hostility if there were siblings as my mother seemed to think there were. Of course, the Cinderella in me would like all my dreams to come true, and that we'd all 'live happily ever after', but I'm realistic enough to know that not ALL dreams come true! If I should find relations it would be nice to become a part of their family, but if not, then so be it. I praised my own self-worth again and told myself it would be their loss.

I knew that many war babies had been devastated, after a long search, to find their fathers were deceased. I had thought this through so many times, but I knew that I must not let it deter me, I must have no regrets.

In February, 1990, Harold Ludwig wrote that he was coming to England again. I felt my spirits rise at the prospect of meeting my 'helper' once more, and began to look forward to his visit. In the meantime, someone had given me the name of a researcher for Stansted Airport and his name was Peter Pallett. I wrote to him immediately, still hoping that I might find my father's name on a list somewhere.

I read Peter's reply. From the way he had written, I could tell he was a nice man. I could feel that he was sincere and would try to help me. He wrote that it was the ninth and not the eighth that was stationed at Stansted at the time I was asking about. I felt confused. My aunt June had said her husband was in the eighth there. Surely she would know? I said to myself.

He went on to comment that he had written to some men who were actually stationed there at that time, maybe they could help me. He told me that there were two reunions held in the States and he would forward my father's name to them, in case someone remembered a Lawrence McCloud. I was grinning to myself and felt very heartened by his letter. Maybe this was the breakthrough I needed, although I was still 'stuck' at that man in Georgia.

Once again my dear friend Harold wrote to me. He had now written to the man in Georgia. I was laughing. I didn't know who had the most tenacity, him or me! I had secretly hoped that he would write, but I didn't like to bother him again, as he had already been so helpful. By that time I had sent my uncle Carl's address book. I was worried that he hadn't received it as there was no mention of it in his letter. I comforted myself with the thought that perhaps our letters had crossed in the post.

Then I had a surprise letter in the post from Pamela Winfield. She wrote requesting my story for a book she was writing on war babies. She asked if I would be interested in submitting a small piece on my search. I felt really excited at that prospect, and eagerly agreed. Pamela forwarded a questionaire.

I sat one evening, when the children were in bed, and studied it. The questions jogged my memory about childhood feelings that had lain buried deep within me. Some of my feelings were so painful that by the time I went to bed that night I felt emotionally drained!

A few weeks later, I was invited over to Pamela's lovely house. She had told me that there would be other war babies there, and on the journey over, I began to get quite excited about meeting them. I had felt as if I was so alone, the only 'war babe' searching for her father. I had always felt so different. It was as if there was something wrong with me, now I was going to meet others who must have experienced some of those same emotions.

I had taken a lot of time choosing what to wear. It had to be the right thing, I thought, as I rummaged through my wardrobe. Finally I settled for something comfortable, but a little on the 'smart' side .

I felt slightly nervous as I entered Pamela's front room, but as I looked around the room at the new friends that I was about to make, I could tell that they were probably feeling just as nervous as I was.

We all chatted away, and I felt myself beginning to relax. Later we went out into the garden for photos to be taken, some of which appeared later in Pamela's book, *'Bye, Bye, Baby'*. Veronica was a new friend that I made that day and it was her father that finally advised me to 'tell it straight' and be honest with our American friends. At that time Veronica had yet to find her dad.

As I stood in the warm sunshine that day thoughts came over me that maybe some good would come out of this book. It might lead to someone giving me a nudge in the right direction. A direction towards my father.

I was thrilled about a few pages of my search being in a book, but I was worried sick at the same time, about my stepfather ever finding out. After all he did not know that I knew he was not my birth father. Since my mother had died, we had subconsciously called an uneasy truce. Friends had found me hard to understand, as I felt sorry for him, even though he had caused me a great deal of unhappiness, and sometimes he had abused me verbally. I knew that he had loved my mother, although it was an unhealthy, possessive love. I knew that in a sense this dark secret surrounding my illicit birth was still with me, as my mother's feelings were still with me, even after her death. I still couldn't be me, these feelings were so strong.

After a very pleasant time at Pamela's, we made our way to meet Harold at his hotel once more. This had been prearranged, and had worked out fine.

Harold and I greeted each other as old friends, and quickly launched into the progress my search had made. He said, "You know, Norma Jean, my wife received a call from Mr McCloud, in Georgia." I gasped! It had been a few months now, and neither Harold or I had heard anything.

He went on,

"He asked for Mr Ludwig, and when she said that I wasn't there, he just went and hung up!" He let out a sigh.

For a second I couldn't believe it, I felt so deflated!

"I was so mad with myself for not being there, now all I can do is hope that he'll ring again." His voice went quiet, I could hear his disappointment.

That man from Georgia, maybe my father, never contacted Harold again.

It was proving for me to be a very frustrating time. This man had called, and in a sense it made me feel a little more hopeful that it could be my father ringing. Maybe he was phoning to say that it was him but that he was unable to tell his family? But I'm his family too, I thought.

Later on, Harold and I and our families and friends, all walked to the local pub. I noticed the white fronted hotels stacked side by side and the busy traffic bustling by, again it all felt so unreal. But luckily photos were taken of another lovely day spent with my kind 'helper' from Missouri. As we said goodbye, I thought, maybe the next time we meet, I will have found my father.

CHAPTER 8

It was August 1990. The children were on holiday from school and we'd all been having a lie in. Realising the time, I'd hurriedly run down the stairs and scooped up the mail that was lying on the mat. As I shuffled through it I noticed Peter Pallet's handwriting.

"I wonder what he's got to say?" I muttered to myself as I walked into the front room. He wrote that he was very sorry, but no one had heard of my father at the reunions. Disappointment flooded over me. He went on, 'It was the 344 bomber group that was stationed at Stansted. At that time it was used as a transit camp for U.S. servicemen at the end of the war.' He then went on to say, that he had found some photos that proved it was the eighth and not the ninth at that time.

My heart sank. Would I ever find my father? Was I really just kidding myself that it would happen? My mother had said that he was four or five years older than she, that would make him about 70 now. The chances of my finding him alive were lessening as the years were passing by. I pictured myself meeting him. What would I say to him if we came face to face? 'Hi Dad?' just like that! For some reason I had begun to feel optimistic again, my imagination was running riot. I would find my father living in a place like 'Southfork' in the T.V. program called 'Dallas'. He would be able to afford to pay for us to visit him every year, no problems financially! My father and I would make up for all those lost years of my childhood without him. I would dream that I found lots of brothers and sisters, nieces and nephews. Family was so important to me, being brought up as an only child. My half-sister, Linda, had died when we were just beginning our journey on the 'path of life' together. Since then I had always felt lonely. I hoped that I had more kinfolk, even if they did dwell in America!

Now all these years later, my life seemed to be turning around. I began to have a strong feeling of self-worth, happiness had eluded me, but now I expected it. The stakes in my life had risen drastically. I promised myself that I would not allow anyone to disrespect me again.

As my expectations had risen, I knew that I had changed. I knew that my marriage was floundering. I felt that my husband prefered to socialise with his friends than be with his family. This caused me a lot anxiety and much sadness at that time.

I was becoming more assertive, so different from the naive young girl of nineteen who stood at the altar full of wonderful dreams inside her. The naive young girl, who felt so 'worldly', truly believing that she and her young husband would live 'happily ever after' if it killed her in the process!

Over twenty years later, emotionally it almost did! I knew that I was not anywhere near reaching my potential. I had a very high mountain to climb, but by God, I would reach the top!

My friend Veronica, who found herself the only child of her G.I. father sent me some newspaper cuttings about Shirley McGlade. She had found her father, and I felt a pang as I read about her happy reunion with him. I commiserated with Shirley as I read her story in her book *"Daddy, Where Are You?"*, and felt that she had been so lucky to have found him still alive.

Reading through the newspaper cuttings, it transpired that in 1986 Shirley had managed to take the American Government to court. She had had the help of America's Public Citizen group, who offered her free advice. She succeeded to go forward and win the case for all G.I. babies. This enabled us to have name, rank, serial number and date of birth. Without this so many would not have been able to make contact with their fathers, and some fathers would not have met their children.

The U.S. Government claims that, 'fatherhood of an illegitimate child during youth is at worst embarrassing, at minimum highly personal.'

obviously, in my opinion, who ever dreamed up that absurd statement, either had no compassion or had definitely not been a part of, or fought in World War Two. I wondered if that person who wrote that, had been separated from his family, thousands of miles from home. Had he experienced the terrifying bombing, wondering if you would survive to ever see your family again.

Meanwhile, Mr McCloud in Georgia had still not answered my letter. Why was this, I wondered? To me his silence was so frustrating. Night after night I would rack my brains as to what on earth I could do to make him respond.

It was suggested to me that maybe I could contact the chief of police in that area. My reasons would be that it was stopping my search; how could I carry on until I got past this man? I thought it was worth a try, so I hurriedly wrote a letter enclosing an international reply coupon, and sent it off. Sadly they never replied.

I decided to write to Shirley McGlade. I felt that it would be sensible to have as many 'fingers' in as many 'pies' as possible. Shirley might just have an idea that I hadn't thought of.

I was begining to feel really down again, as grave doubts kept sweeping over me. Was it all worth it? I asked myself again. Emotionally, I was having a tough time at home. I was fearful for the future; what did it hold for me? I knew that I was going to have to be strong.

I thought about my search. For many years now, I'd looked for someone that lived somewhere in the United States of America. A man, who, if I found him in the end, might reject me, just as I felt I had been rejected all my life. Well, I said to myself, should I stop now before I self-inflict any more pain?

I would look at myself in the mirror, scrutinising my face for signs of aging. I would ask myself, what if you got to sixty or seventy, and looked back, and wished that you had continued on and found your father? I knew for certain then, that I had to carry on. That I must have no regrets.

In between all this I had been thinking about Harold Ludwigs kindness to me and decided to send him a present. He very quickly replied, thanking me, and then immediately lapsed into comments about Georgia.

'Do not be tempted to jump on a plane, and make your way to this man's front door. It would be a highly dangerous thing to do! So many people in America have fire-arms, this man might even have one and be so mad at you, he might even fire it!' At one point during our letter-writing Harold sent me a leaflet on 'Camping in Georgia', I laughed at that, but I also knew that the reality of me actually knocking on this man's front door was not a possibility.

As I sat and thought deeply about my search, I would think about my mother. She had to bear this all alone, without the support of my natural father. It was at a time, when these things were thought to be very bad, a strong stigma to bear. She didn't get into this alone, I wasn't the product of an immaculate conception, was I? I was the one who ultimately paid the price. Tears filled my eyes and sadness overwhelmed me as I thought about it.

I was now so high on my pedestal, that for the first time I thought, if I ever get to meet my father, he will be very, very proud of me.

One evening I sat on the floor with my search papers scattered all around me. What on earth shall I do next, I asked myself? I leafed through them and my eyes seemed to rest on an old letter from the National Personnel Records Center, in Missourri. I knew it had been a long time since I had written to them, they must have some sort of record there about my father. I know that there was this fire in 1973, but surely they must have at least my father's name, and perhaps a serial number, or something? My father couldn't have disappeared altogether. I reasoned that a record of all the men that served in the Second World War must be in that building somewhere. If only I could get on a plane and fly to St. Louis, Missouri! What I'd give to spend two days, just two days in that building. I would sit at one of their computers, until I came up with a Lawrence McCloud who fitted the bill. Mum had said March 1946, I would look for that. My research would not stop anyone else from doing their job, would it?

I was exasperated with it all. I was caught seemingly in a 'catch 22' situation. I knew that I couldn't give up; then my commonsense would overide my temporary insanity about flying to St. Louis. Where would I get the money for my flight and my lodgings? Then who would look after the children while I was thousands of miles away?

It was now December 1990. I had written to the NPRC that night and now I had their reply. They commented that, 'They were physical custodians of the military records, whether they were retired or deceased.'

The letter continued on yet again, about the fire in 1973. I knew that this fire had actually happened, but at the same time,

I felt that they had used this excuse with me too many times! Again I was feeling really depressed, a lump came up in my throat, as I put my head in my hands!

CHAPTER 9

It was now 1991. What is in store for me this New Year? Would this year be the year that I would find my elusive G.I. soldier father?

It was now five years since I'd learned of my father, and almost three years since my mother had died. Time had been the healer, as everyone who has lost someone understands, but I still missed her so much.

I could not believe how the years had flown. I was still going through my papers, looking for another idea, another pathway to follow. I had come across an address for a group called BOTNA. I realised it was the address of another researcher, this time in Suffolk, in England. I was still on the track of trying to find my father's unit, still trying to find a list which held my father's name. I wrote a letter of enquiry.

An answer came back, reinforcing Peter Pallett's, the researcher for Stansted, that it was indeed the 344 bomber group at Stansted.

Shortly after that, I received a very sad letter from Peter Pallett's wife informing me that he had suddenly passed away. Although I had never actually met Peter, he had been most helpful to me, and I felt very saddened at the news.

Peter's wife passed on the name of the new researcher, Reg Robinson. She had also enclosed his phone number.

I immediately telephoned Reg, explaining to him about my

search. I could hear his enthusiasm, and knew that he would try to help me. Reg and I became firm friends in the coming years, right up to this day.

One day Reg came to my house with a briefcase full of memorabilia from Stansted. I felt excited as he withdrew old photos of the men stationed at Stansted during the War years. I grabbed them up one at a time, peering at them, trying to see my uncle Carl's face there. Maybe I might see Larry, after all I had seen a photo of my father. I felt that I would recognize him. I wasn't lucky that day, but Reg carried on trying to help with suggestions of other ideas all the time.

There were reunions at Stansted which Reg would organize. I was amazed at the atmosphere as I and my friends arrived. It was just like stepping back in time to the War years. Some people were dressed up in the 'forties' style and were 'jitterbugging' to the Glen Miller sound. What really made the evening so spectacular was the appearance of the ageless 'Beverley Sisters' singing all those poignant war time songs.

During the evening we were plunged into darkness and the sirens would wail. Our imaginations would soar as the drone of 'aeroplanes' sounded above our heads! Search lights shone out, looking for pretend 'planes' in an imaginary 'sky'.

Once there, I would have this impulse to grab the microphone, and tell everyone of my story, just in case there was somebody there who might remember a Lawrence McCloud.

Back home, it was time to get on with my search. Harold had written. Once more he had enclosed leaflets on camping in Georgia. He wrote that he was going on holiday and for two pins he'd come back via Georgia. I knew that he was joking, but I realised that we both shared the desire to knock on this man's door. He'd also enclosed a map of Georgia. I knelt down on the carpet, and spread the map out on the floor in front of me. I looked hard at the area where I thought this Mr McCloud lived. I put my finger there and traced it across, trying to find the nearest airport. If he were my father, I'd better be prepared to travel very quickly. I said to myself.

I smiled as I imagined myself actually camping in Georgia, my small tent pitched out on some grassy plain, exposing myself to all kinds of danger, I thought. I'd have to cook on an open fire, thinking all the time of some crazy plan to meet my father. I got up and played the music to 'Somewhere Out There' again, thinking, well, at least we would be on the same land, sleeping underneath the same big sky!

In Harold's letter, he finally mentioned my uncle's diary. 'Once back from his vacation, he would get down to that.'

Mentally I had reached an all time low. I felt so hopeless. I was struggling to keep my home and my family on an even keel, and yet this was taking all my emotional energy. Again I asked myself if I should let my search go. What was the point, would I really find my father? There was still this part of me that felt it was still unreal. It was hard to let go of that forty year old lie that I had been living all my life. I wasn't even sure if I had the right spelling of his surname. My father probably wasn't still alive. It was no good, I'd have to leave it for a while.

A couple of weeks went by; I began to think about it again. I talked to myself. Are you going to let this thing beat you, even though you have turmoil in your life? I knew that deep down, something was spurring me on, telling me that I would find him, and I would find him alive.

I felt like a juggler must feel, juggling my life, trying to keep everyone happy, the children, my job, the house. I needed to find the other half of my jigsaw puzzle. I needed to feel complete, whatever I might find at the end of it. I felt as if I wasn't even half-way up my mountain.

May 1991. Harold had written about my uncle Carl's wartime diary. He wrote, that he had been through it with a fine tooth comb. He had tried to phone everyone in there, but had no luck. After all it was over forty years old.

"Thanks for trying, Harold," I said aloud.

I was still 'stuck' at this man in Georgia. It was so frustrating. How could I get past him if he wasn't the man I was looking for; my father. Suddenly I thought, I wrote to a social worker in Kansas, why don't I do the same now? I smiled to myself. So I wrote a carefully worded letter, explaining everything and sent it to the County Hall, Savanna, Georgia, enclosing the usual, International reply coupon. Now I might get somewhere. Somehow, I felt a little better this time, a bit different.

I had still been writing intermittently to my McCloud directory, but I was filled with depression when there were no replies. I often wondered what these people did with their International reply coupons. It was about a month later, when I noticed on the front door mat, a letter in my own handwriting. I frowned, when it suddenly came to me that it was one of my self-addressed envelopes! I rushed to open it. My heart fluttered as I realised that it was my own letter that I had written to the social worker, and there were some comments on the bottom of it.

This lady wrote that she was from the CW support service. I felt stunned. I continued to read on. 'This man is not the person you are looking for. He is black, aged 65, and never been out of the States!'

I couldn't believe what I was reading. Black, this man is black? I moved towards the nearest chair and slowly sank into it. After all this time? It wasn't fair, not after all this time?

I gripped the arms of the chair. I was beginning to feel angry! How rude of this man, not to let me know this? Then an element of doubt crept into my mind. How do I know this is true? Could this Mr McCloud have written on the letter himself? I wouldn't know, would I? I slowly turned the letter over. There on the back was the official stamp, and a phone number, almost as if the social worker had read my mind.

I passed my hand over my forehead, feeling a wry smile coming on, as I began to see the funny side of it! That's really ironic, I said to myself. A whole year 'stuck' at a man who turns out to be black! That would happen to me. No wonder he never answered my letters, and all those reply coupons? I let out a big sigh. Now I'm back to square one again!

In the beginning I had serious doubts about this man. "I should have gone with my instincts," I muttered to myself, as I flicked on the switch of the kettle.

Well, it looks like it's back to Kansas, I thought, as I poured myself a strong cup of tea. I'll give that another go. That man, my father, is out there somewhere !

Norma Jean's mother, Edna

Norma Jean's father, Lawrence McCloud

Somewhere Out There

Lawrence McCloud on far right. Taken in Holland, 1944.

SOMEWHERE OUT THERE

9th Air Force

8th Air Force

Photograph by Reg Robinson

Huts at Stansted Airport during the Second World War

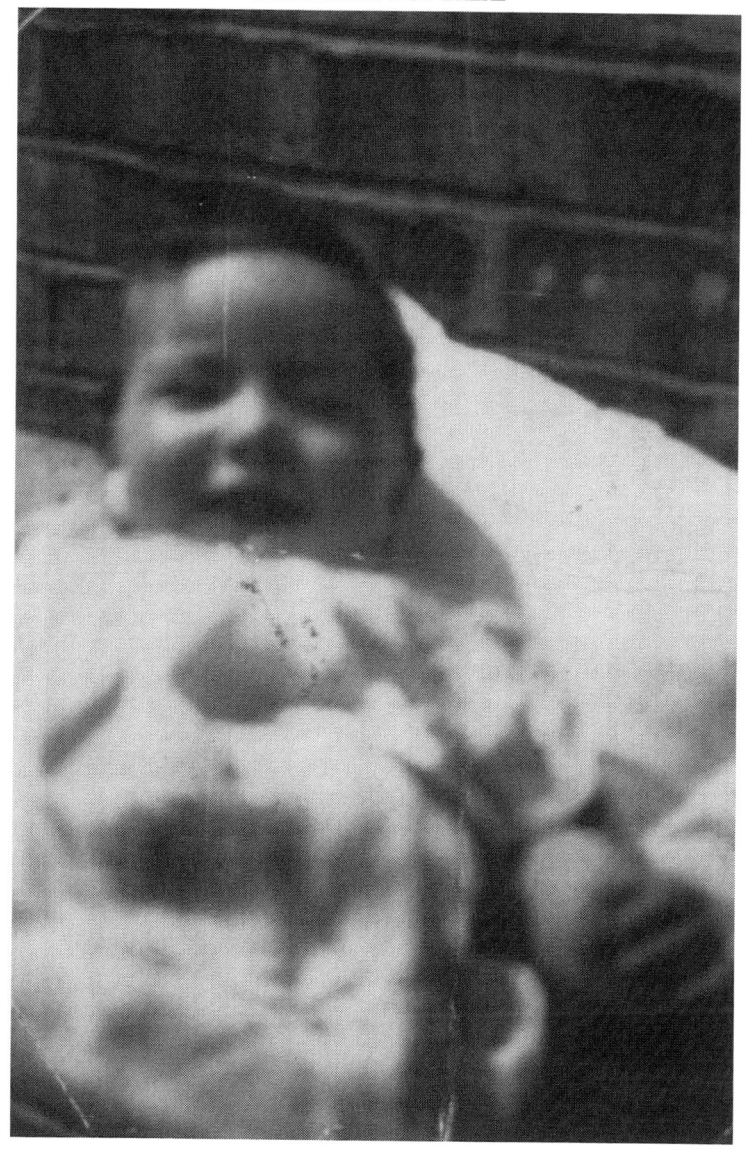

*The only known photo in existence
of Norma Jean as a baby in 1946*

1944
June and Joan
Norma's twin-sister aunts

1945
Norma's Aunt June, June's husband, Carl (Larry's 'buddie'), with their baby son, Gary.

As Children:
*Norma (on the right) with Aunt Sandra,
who suggested that Larry might be her father.*

*Norma Jean (left) with her half-sister, Linda,
who died of a heart complaint at the age of seven.*

Florida, 1989
Aunt June (who married her GI) with Hayley and Adam.
"There are alligators in that river"!

Norma Jean with Pamela Winfield, founder of TRACE.

SOMEWHERE OUT THERE

Harold Ludwig, my 'helper' in Missouri

*Norma Jean with Philip Grinton,
who met her in San Francisco*

*Norma Jean with her friend, Chris Nicholson,
who helped her over her 'final hurdle'.*

*Norma Jean with Barbara Cowin (left) and Anita Verender,
also G.I. babies*

CHAPTER 10

After receiving the shocking news from the social worker, in Savanna, Georgia, I hurriedly wrote a brief note to Pamela Winfield and Harold Ludwig. I knew that Pamela's book had gone to print and so it was too late for my ending in Georgia.

It was nice to think that a few pages of my search were going into a book, as I was now back to the beginning as far as I was concerned!

Meanwhile, I had to keep busy, I had to do something. I decided to write again to the National Personnel Record Center in St. Louis. They forwarded me yet another form to fill in, which I did promptly and returned it to them. By April they had returned it once more, requesting more information. They required name, rank, serial number, date of birth. They then asked if he were deceased.

"Who's sending me these ridiculous questions? If I knew the answers, I wouldn't be writing to you, would I?" I said, now gripping the form, like I'd like to grip the Military!

How I was going to break through the mighty barrier of the Military, I just did not know.

I sat at the table the next morning, my chin cupped in my hands, thinking over all my options. My father was on that computer somewhere, he had to be. He was on that computer at the NPRC somewhere. He was my father and I had a right to know if he were dead or alive. None of this was my fault. The scales of justice were unevenly balanced; It was not fair! It was my business to know where he was, and it was his right to know about me. He should have the choice, so should all the G.I. fathers, to know their children, if they want to. This was nothing to do with the surrogate personnel of the Military. It felt to me, at that time, that these unknown faces of the Military were behaving like Gods with my life! My life! They were deciding my fate, for I knew the answer lay with them, behind the doors of the National Personnel Records Center, St. Louis, Missouri.

"Well, we'll soon see," I said aloud, through gritted teeth.

At about the same time, someone else had mentioned writing to the veterans in Washington. If I enclosed a letter to my father in an unsealed envelope, they would forward it to the veteran. I thought this was worth a go, so I promptly followed the instructions and posted it off. I felt cynical at that time and wondered if my letter would ever reach him. I had heard that most of these letters ended up in someone's tidy bin, beneath some desk, in some office, somewhere.

I began to imagine my father receiving my letter. On opening it, I sensed he would get a terrible shock, but what else could I do? I had to make contact with him or his children somehow.

What if my father had emigrated and never actually lived in America any more? I pushed those thoughts to the back of my mind, I knew that I was wavering again, but I also knew in my heart of hearts that I must continue. I felt as if I were on a train hurtling forward, and that I would eventually stop, when I reached my destination!

I had received two letters about the man in Georgia. One from Harold and the other from Shirley McGlade. Harold commented, 'No wonder he never replied,' and Shirley also ran a check for me.

Shirley reminded me again, that the American wife more often than not opened all the mail. I frowned with concern as I thought that maybe my father's wife opened this one from the veterans. My imagination was running riot!

In July 1991, a letter plopped onto the mat that took me by surprise. It was a very rare reply from my McCloud directory. I hurried into the front room, eager to read it! It was a relative of an E. McCloud. He wrote, 'I am very sorry but he isn't the man you are looking for. Also this man has Alzheimer's disease.

I looked at the letter, what if my father has this disease? What if he has some other genetic disease, and I was liable to inherit it? I had visions of my father in a sanatorium somewhere. As I slowly walked towards him, he wouldn't show any response to me. How would I feel about that? I had pictured that scenerio and worked through them in my mind. I kept telling myself, that whatever happened I had to be prepared for it.

How funny! At last there were replies to my McCloud directory, now I had another. This Mr McCloud had commented that there was no Lawrence in his family, but was I sure that I had the right spelling? I felt nervous when I read that. What if after all these years I had the incorrect spelling? I broke out in a sweat. I thought of my mother, I could hear her voice, just as it was that day on the telephone, spelling out my father's name. Why did she spell it? Even after all this time, I still didn't trust her. If I ended up never finding him, then I would wonder about that spelling for the rest of my life.

Shortly after that I had a letter returned from my directory unopened. I felt a real fear. What if this one were my father, and he wanted nothing to do with me? There was a message stamped on the envelope, from the postmaster, that stated, 'this person has moved'. I imagined that this actually was my father and he had moved because of me. The thought that he was rejecting me, was unbearable then, but later I came to terms with those thoughts, and decided it would be his loss!

I wrote a hasty letter to the postmaster. I had been advised to send a dollar and ask for my letter to be forwarded to the latest address. It was really ironic. The US postal service forwarded my letter, and this turned out to be the Mr McCloud in Kansas! He had retired and moved away. I felt awful for bothering them once more, and hoped that they would understand.

It was October 15th. At last I had received a letter from the Veterans' Affairs. They had taken a long time to reply and I was beginning to feel uneasy.

Did the Military Personnel not realise just how important this was? Am I the only person in the whole wide world who is searching for her father? (Well thats what it felt like!) Why are they not giving my letters the immediate attention that they deserve? This is life and death here, my life, my fate, and most importantly my future.

I received a standard letter from the Veterans, informing me 'that they had forwarded my letter to the Veteran'. I felt heartened by that response, as I had been told that they would tell me if he were dead.

That letter gave me a slight ray of hope. They must know who and where he is then, I said to myself. This means that he is alive. My heart went into my mouth as I had this strong feeling again that I would find him one day. I noticed that the letter was signed by a Mrs Byers. Perhaps this lady had a compassionate nature? What if I phoned her, and put my case to her in a most polite way? I felt a wave of guilt, as I really couldn't afford to phone America, then I said to myself, what's money to life?

I fumbled as I dialled the number, I wasn't used to speaking to strangers, especially long distance. I gripped the receiver hard as I listened to the strange dull and monotonous tone of the U.S. phone. Suddenly a man with a strong American accent answered, "Veterans office."

"Hello, this is Norma Jean Clarke, from England. Could I speak to Mrs Byers, please?" I let out a breath.

The phone was muffled, as he put his hand over the mouthpiece, but I could still hear him faintly.

"I'm afraid she's too busy to come to the phone, can I help you?"

Feeling deflated, I quickly explained who I was and for whom I was searching. I felt agitated, the longer I was on the phone, the more it was going to cost me.

Again I heard this man put his hand over the mouthpiece.

"Have you phoned Mr McCloud, John?" A woman's voice which I took to be Mrs Byers.

"Yes, I have." He said.

"Okay, tell Mrs Clarke, that we can't help her any more." My heart sank.

This man, John, did not realise that I had heard his muffled conversation. He related her message to me and we said goodbye. I stood still beside the telephone and felt puzzled. I had this strange feeling, a 'sixth sense' that Mrs Byers had spoken loudly on purpose. Maybe I was wrong about that, but my hunches were usually right.

Later that evening it began to dawn on me. They had phoned a Mr McCloud, and this man was alive. Surely they wouldn't telephone someone unless they were reasonably sure, would they?

My friend who had found her G.I. father told me that the Veterans had phoned her father three times before he responded. My spirits rose at that thought. So they do try after all? I smiled to myself.

CHAPTER 11

I peered into the mirror and found to my dismay, yet another grey hair! How time is going by I thought, and I don't like it! To think when I was a lot younger I used to wish it away!

It was now November 1991. I could see the future for me alone with my children. When would I be happy? I asked myself.

I knew one thing that would make me sublimely happy and that would be to meet my father.

I looked down at the letter in my hand. It was another from the National Personnel Record Center in Missouri. Once again they reminded me of the fire there in 1973 that destroyed 80% of all records. The letter continued that they could find no trace of a L. McCloud.

This puzzled me. How can this be? I had already received three 'L. McClouds' from them. I had their names, ranks and serial numbers. One of these was that man in Georgia. So they must have records of some sort. I had worked with computers in a bank for sixteen years. I knew that whoever had completed that search, hadn't searched deeply enough. They *must* have the names of every man that served in the Second World War.

Surely they would have back-up lists elsewhere too?

I turned over the page. The letter continued, referring to the 'freedom of information act', and a person's right to it. The letter referred to comments that I had made in my last letter.

Saying, was I aware that there was nothing that they could release to me. The court order allows the Veterans to release the name, rank, serial number, marital status, dependents, rank/grade, salary, civilian educational level, decorations and awards, duty status, a photograph, court marshals, separation and induction.

For Veterans known to be deceased, it permits the home address and the place of burial and the letter finished with informing me once more that they were very sorry that they could not help me as they had no record of my father.

I read the letter through again, trying to digest exactly what they meant. My immediate reaction to it was that of mistrust. So that meant then, that if any of us War babies wrote to them requesting knowledge of our biological fathers they could actually tell us that they had no knowledge of them? How would we know if that was the truth? Later, the instinct that I had, proved to be right, but at the time I felt devastated! I had always felt that the Military held the key to finding my father. I thought about the man who penned this letter. Maybe he did not agree to fathers being found. Perhaps he'd used his own emotions, and he'd put himself in a father's position and used these feelings to influence his letter to me. This was something that I would never know. My search, and my problems in my personal life were overwhelming me! Deflated, I felt that I would have to let go of my search. I felt that I was on the brink of a nervous collapse, everything seemed against me. I felt mentally fatigued, drained and what was the point of carrying on?

Suddenly, fate seemed to intervene and interrupt my despondency. I received a heartening letter from Harold. His letter focused on encouragement, not to give up. It was so uncanny, almost as if he'd known about my feelings by telepathy all the way across the ocean!

It was Christmas time again, and I made up my mind that whatever happened it would be a great one for the children, and it was. Somehow I got through it, and emerged into the New Year, with feelings of a fresh start. After all that hard work, and that of my friends, the helpers, was I just going to let that go? Hadn't I always told myself that I would never let it beat me, that I must have no regrets? People had expectations of me, what was I going to do, let them all down? It would all be for nothing.

I sat back at my desk, sifting through my letters from the Military. Some time before, the National Personnel Record Center had sent me information on three L. McClouds. One had been that man in Georgia, another had died in 1971. I felt sad as I read his details, and thought again that my own father might be dead as well. I realised that he was not this man, as his dates of enlistment and separation did not tie in with my conception. I felt relieved, even though I might have to face bad news myself at the end of my search. All the time I was on the lookout for a breakthrough. I felt that the key factor was my father going back to the States in March 1946. Then, profound thoughts would sweep over me. Would I ever see my father's face, even if I didn't like what I saw?

I picked up the third man's details, this man's record of service seemed to be too short, and I doubted that he was the one. Still it was worth writing to Harold and asking his opinion. He quickly replied.

'My contact said that there was a folder on this man who you are enquiring about. My contacts name is Charles Pelligrini. It would be a good idea to write to him personally, he said that maybe he could help.'

I felt a slow smile spreading across my face, and thought, someone from the Military is actually offering to help me? Surely this is the best news yet. I still felt that for me, personally, the Military was the best way to go.

Little did I know then, what a great part Charles Pelligrini would be playing in helping me find my father.

I immediately sat down at the table, and wrote a hasty letter to this man. I knew that I was going to have to draw on all my reserves of patience again, and just wait for his reply. I hated to bother anyone as I knew these people were very busy, but at the end of the day, this was the most important thing to me. This was my life, my future happiness. For once I needed to be selfish, I had to get on and finish this, for better or for worse.

Whilst I was still waiting for my reply, I noticed much to my surprise, a letter on the mat from the McCloud directory. As I walked back down the hall it seemed strange, as it always did, opening an envelope that was written in my own handwriting. At least I always knew where the letter was coming from.

I began to read the letter, and immediately felt a pang of guilt! It turned out to be from a lady who wrote, 'my deceased brother was unfortunately killed in an accident, but he was not the man you are looking for.'

I sat down feeling dreadful for bothering this lady in a quest to find my father. She was so nice to take the trouble to even reply to me at that time. For the rest of the day it troubled me, but I consoled myself with the thoughts, how was I to know? I placed the letter carefully in the folder along with the others, and taking a deep breath, pulled myself up, and began once more to focus on my task.

Around the same time I received a letter from Jane, another War baby. 'Was I really sure that this man was black? How did I know this? Had I got proof? It could be a ruse to put me of the track!'

This letter had reiterated my own thoughts, but I had sifted through all these things and in the end come to the conclusion, that I would have to start to trust at some point. How could I move on otherwise? I knew in my heart of hearts that the man in Georgia was not the one.

As time was going, I felt that my confidence in finding my father was going too. I seemed to have lost faith in myself. What if it was the wrong spelling of the surname? I broke out in a cold sweat at the thought of that. Why on earth did my mother spell it out to me when she needn't have done? It seemed such a strange thing for her to do after keeping this secret for forty years! What if it was the wrong spelling? What if she'd spelt it out wrongly on purpose? What would I do? I felt tears come to my eyes. There would be no choice, I would have to start all over again!

I began making a mental list. I would have to write to all those people all over again! I'd have to get a different McCloud directory, but which spelling would I choose? I'd have to re-write to the Military, again filling in all those forms! I wiped my eyes, I couldn't bear the thought of it.

What could I do now? I asked myself. Perhaps it would be a good idea if I spoke to Mr Pelligrini personally. Maybe I could appeal to the compassionate part of him that I felt sure every Military man possessed underneath his skin. I decided that I would speak to him. I would try to get over to him the urgency of my search. Time was running out! Maybe if he heard the desperation in my voice, he might just take pity on me and help me that little bit more.

I hurried to the phone and before I could change my mind, dialled the number. Once again I was very conscious of the money and what this was going to cost me. I quickly brushed those thoughts to the side, held my breath and waited for someone to answer?

At last I was speaking to Mr Pelligrini. I explained in detail just who I was, and so relieved when I realised he was so understanding and would try to help. I had mentioned that a short part of my story was in a book, and felt very happy as our transatlantic call ended with a promise that he would do all he could. Smiling to myself I slowly replaced the receiver, at the same time feeling a satisfaction that I hadn't felt before. Was this an omen? I asked myself.

Less than a week later I received a letter from Mr Pelligrini. The thickness of the letter arriving surprised me, and my heart fluttered when I realised that he had actually done the research for it himself. Excitement rose in me as I began to read his letter. At first I couldn't quite take in the importance of it. Gradually a warm feeling started in my toes and began to slowly waft over me. My jaw dropped open, as I realised that I had made a breakthrough! I turned and hurried into the lounge, and spread the letter out on the table. The letter stated,

1) In our records locator system, there are fifteen Lawrence McClouds. Two of these have no middle initial, and you have the information supplied to you already.

2) Of the thirteen remaining Veterans, three were in the United States Navy.

3) Of the ten remaining veterans, three were in the United States Army or Airforce, but not during World War Two.

4) I have provided you with the information on the three remaining Veterans. The records of these three remaining men were destroyed in the fire of 1973, and other than the addresses of 1945/46, we have no further information available that we are witholding. All these men were World War Two Veterans, but you will note that two of the three were discharged prior to March 1946.'

I felt a tightness in my chest! This letter seemed unreal to me. I couldn't believe that I had actually got something positive at last! I looked back at the letter I held shakily in my hand. It continued,

'The only remaining man was L.H. McCloud, service number 39721917, since you are unable to supply much information on Mr McCloud, and have very little information to match that which you have provided, I can't say with certainty that this is the man you are looking for.'

I slowly sank down into the armchair, gripping the side of the table as I sat down. Once more my head seemed to be spinning. I gulped as I read the last sentence again and again. How long I had waited for a breakthrough? Anything, any slightest thing, that might help me find my father. At last I held that information in my hand, and it came, as I always thought it would, from the Military! My eyes travelled down the page, and my hands shook as I read this man's date of separation'. It said March 1946! I felt my stomach do a somersault. There it was, in black and white! I had searched for this for so many years, and now I had the dates that my mother had spoken about, so long ago. If she hadn't said those words, "He went back to the States in March 1946." There couldn't be two L. McCloud's sent back to the States in March 1946, could there? It must be him!

I jumped out of my chair and danced around the room!

Breathlessly I went back to look at the letter again. My eyes travelled down the paper, resting on the part that said, city/town/residence. I stared wide-eyed as I read, Kansas City, Missouri. March 1946.

There it was, it all tied in! My aunt's suggestion of Kansas. This man had both these pieces of information on one piece of paper. There was no getting away from it, it had to be him!

I continued to read on. It said, 'Induction/separation, Riverside, California, Jefferson Barracks, Missouri.'

For a minute I frowned, what does this mean? Does this mean that this man entered the U.S. Army at California and was demobbed at Missouri, or the other way around? Although this puzzled me, I shelved that thought for the moment. I felt so excited.

Suddenly I felt very strong, invigorated! Nothing was going to stand in my way now! I would continue to push until I got this L.H. McCloud's address. Mr Pelligrini had been absolutely wonderful. I would write to him again, and ask if he had anything more for me. At last I could see a light at the end of the tunnel. Nothing would stop me now!

CHAPTER 12

The publication of Pamela's book was imminent. I had received my invitation and as it was the first one that I had ever been to, let alone been a part of, it was really exciting for me. I puffed out with pride at the thought of it. How different I was now, all this way 'down the road', I thought.

I saw myself as just an ordinary person, with an extraordinary story, one that I never knew anything about until I reached the age of forty. I felt so different, I never seemed to fit in. I spoke to my friend Barbara of this, and as she is another War babe, she nodded her head in total agreement.

"Maybe we all come from Atlantis?" she commented and we both laughed, but who knows?

I had never been to the Imperial War Museum, where we had to go for the publication, but I was really looking forward to seeing it.

I'd been panicking about what to wear, but at last a friend altered a suit, and matched a blouse to it, and I was ready to go!

At the time I had been very worried about my stepfather's reaction, should he find out about this.

He still wasn't aware then, that I knew that he was not my biological father. It seems funny to me now, that I ever thought like that, as I have finally severed the ties with him. I left far behind me his Victorian dominance of which I was always so afraid. It is hard for me to put into words the anxiety I felt, as a child, when his key went into the front door lock. But back then in 1992, I tried to forgive, but now I know you can never forget.

Now, I was walking up the stone steps and entering into the musty smelling building of the Imperial War Museum. I felt so excited and important. A stage troupe were dressed as G.I.'s, and the girls in their 40's costume's were jitterbugging. It really set the scene. I could sense the War time days, as if I'd been transported back in time. I glanced around at the old Wartime planes, and the battered tanks. It was hard to believe that they had once fought a war.

I looked around and noticed other War-babies there, some that I knew and some that I didn't. We all chatted together, all with a common bond. At last reality took over and I had the book clasped firmly in my hands. That day marked yet another turning point for Norma Jean.

Now it was time to get back to my search, and to try to fathom out how on earth I was going to obtain this Lawrence McCloud's address.

I tried to think about a wider aspect of my search. Was there anything that I hadn't tried, anything that I hadn't thought of? After lots of deliberation, I decided to write again to the Veterans Affairs, Washington. Washington was their head office. If anyone would be able to trace this L. H. McCloud, surely the head office could? I wrote my letter as if it were actually going to reach my father. I imagined him receiving it and visualized him opening and reading its contents. Of course this was fantasy, how would I ever know if it was really going to reach my father? or even if he were still alive? I folded the letter carefully and placed it into an envelope. I did not seal the envelope in order to allow anyone at the Veterans to verify that I was indeed searching for my father. Once again I sent it off.

At the same time I had been waiting for a reply from Mr

Pelligrini, pertaining to whether or not he could find any more information that might help me? At last his reply came; impatiently I grappled at the contents. My heart went out to him in gratitude when I realised what he had enclosed.

'The only record available for Mr L. H. McCloud, was his last pay-slip voucher.' I took a quick glance at it and felt excitement rise in me. I stared fascinated. This was only a photocopy, but the pay-slip itself was so old, a part of history. I imagined this man, perhaps my father, arriving wearily at his home town, a vastly different man to the youth that had left some years before. How the war would have changed him, changed every aspect of his life, his views, his expectations for his future.

I studied the pay-slip, there was so much to look at. I decided to be methodical and start at the top. In the top left hand box were the names, Mr and Mrs Lutman. The address had been blanked out. Obviously the Military had done this, and I tutted with annoyance. I moved across to the light and held it up, hoping that I would be able to develop x-ray eyes!

My curiosity about this was aroused. My mother had told me that when Larry went back to the States, he had lived with his mother, and waited for her to join him. Whether this was actually true or not, I doubted that I would ever know. Perhaps the name Lutman was his mother's name? Maybe she re-married? It was all very puzzling?

Mr Pelligrini wrote that he would forward a letter for me to the address on the pay-slip, but he could not guarantee that it would reach them. He suggested that I should place another letter in an unsealed envelope, and then place this in turn in a sealed envelope. He would send this off, and if it was returned, he would place it on Mr McCloud's file. If I should never trace him, then one day when my father was deceased, at least his relatives would be informed of me. I felt really pleased about this, and silently thanked him. I turned my attention back to the payslip. It was only a photocopy, and some of the print was illegible. Screwing my eyes up I could just make out the date, March 1946. I could see the words Kansas, MO. My eyes then drifted down to the payment section. I noticed that his last payment was fifty dollars. I thought again about this soldier, Lawrence McCloud, and his last pay-slip. It must have seemed such a vast amount of money to him. I mentally pictured this man leaving the barracks for the very last time. His life must have been in turmoil, wondering what he was going to do.

Finally my eyes came to rest on this man's signature written almost half a century ago. Most probably this man was my father, and he had signed this piece of paper that I held shakily in my hand. I put the wage slip down on the table and traced with my forefinger over the signature, trying to 'sense' if it were actually my father's handwriting. I tried to draw once again, on my psychic ability, my 'sixth sense' that I felt I had.

Suddenly I saw again in my 'mind's eye', that large photograph in my grandmother's house when I was a child. I 'pictured' his writing, the letter 'L' was shaped in the same way as this one on the pay slip. I remembered again that it had said, 'All my love Larry.' Although my net was closing in, the reality of what I might face was slowly sinking in. What if, when I found my father and we made contact, what if he were an alcoholic? How would I feel, if coming face to face, he was reeling from too much drink? I would probably only meet him once in my life anyway. I didn't have the money to travel to America every year. Then I thought, what if he were disabled? Well, that wouldn't bother me one little bit, especially if he wanted to meet me. I suddenly felt very profound, thinking deeply about how I would feel if he did actually reject me? I paled as I thought about coping with that rejection. I'd had this all my life, or from as far back as I could remember, from the man that I had thought of as my father for forty years. He had never wanted me, and I had always known it. Eventually I sifted through all these feelings and gradually came to terms with them. I knew my self-worth now.

In June 1992, I received another letter from the NPRC. My letter to Mr and Mrs Luteman had been undeliverable and now it had been placed on Mr McCloud's file. I sighed, it was as I expected, however, Mr Pelligrini must think that this is the man I'm searching for, or would he do such a positive thing? I doubted it and smiled at the thought. Well, I comforted myself, if I never met my father, at least his family would know one day.

I was sure now, that this was the man I was looking for, and yet the reality of that, after all the years of searching for him, had still not really sunk in on me. I felt nervous, how could I get his address? What if I never found out where he lived! What on earth could I do next? I picked up my magazine, called 'How to Locate a Buddie', and leafed through it. Suddenly I spotted a section about the Drivers Licensing Bureau. I read that for ten dollars they will run a check for you. That would be a good idea, I thought, and quickly sent off a letter of enquiry. Sadly, their reply was disappointing. They needed the missing person's date of birth. They had also stopped doing this kind of check for the general public, but if I cared to put a letter in an unsealed envelope? I thought, oh no, not again! I felt as if I was hitting my head against a brick wall. It seemed as if I was going round and round in circles. I had felt so hopeful with this and yet once again my hopes were dashed!

Won't someone help a daughter find a father, before it's too late? I said again.

Well, if that way is not going to get me through my father's front door, then I would have to try some other way. My head was pounding, and yet at the same time I tried to look at it philosophicaly. My life, and the way it has been, had made me the strong woman that I have become. I am a born fighter, especially if I believe in anything.

After the let down of the Drivers License Bureau, it slowly dawned on me that I did need this man's date of birth. I felt extremely weary of it all. I knew that it would mean another struggle to gain this information. My mind was flitting from one idea to another, but it still kept returning to one name, Charles Pelligrini.

On a sudden impulse, I hurried to the phone, picked it up and quickly dialled America. I had now acquired Charles Pelligrini's direct line, straight to his desk. I shrugged of the slight niggle of the cost of another transatlantic telephone call, as I listened to the dull, slow tone as it rang.

"Hello."

"Hello, is that Charles Pelligrini," I said breathlessly.

"Yes, who is it?" he sounded puzzled.

As I explained who I was, he quickly realised and said, "I wrote to you, did you get my letter?" He sounded so pleasant.

"Yes, thank you very much, I'm glad that my letter is now on Mr McCloud's file, that's wonderful! I know that he is the one." Then I quickly asked. "I have heard that you have a copy of Pamela's book?"

"Yes, I do. It's right here on my desk."

I smiled, "Well, a part of my story is in that book, plus my photograph." I felt so pleased. Maybe, just maybe this will help me.

"Right I'll look for the page."

I felt a nervous giggle rise up in my throat, as I thought, this is a strange way to meet someone.

"I've got your picture, it's real nice to know who I'm talking to."

I have always felt that phone call, that day, really helped me. I plucked up the courage and said, "Mr Pelligrini, you have helped me so much, is there anything, anything else that you could find out for me, please? Is there anyway that you could get this man's date of birth?" I exhaled, I had said it!

"I do not believe that it is in his file, but I will go and check for you. I will write to you."

"Thank you very much, Mr Pelligrini. Thank you again for everything you have done for me."

As we said goodbye, I drew a deep breath, and felt a real sense of satisfaction.

As I put the phone down, I turned and looked into the mirror. I wondered as I studied my eyes and the black sweep of my eyebrows, whether I looked like this man, Larry, my biological father. I certainly hoped that I wouldn't be too much older before we met. I had visions of myself, totally grey-haired, and teetering on a walking stick, the rate my search was going! I felt a pang as I thought about not knowing Larry as a child. But at least there's a chance of knowing him now.

A few days later I had a conversation with Shirley McGlade, the person who took the U.S. Government to court. She suggested that I write again to the Veterans' Affairs, but this time to ask for this man's date of birth. She said that I was to quote the 'freedom of Information Act' to them. I groaned inwardly at the thought of writing to them yet again, but said silently, 'no pain, no gain!' I wrote straight away.

It was July 1992, when I got a very formal reply from the Veterans' Office.

'Your request for Mr L.H. McCloud's date of birth is denied.' I stared at the letter, beginning to feel angry.

'It is covered by the systems of records that are covered by the secrets act. It was considered under title 5, section 5 2a(b). No exception could be found that would allow the V. A. to allow this man's date of birth. We considered your request under the 'freedom of information act, that also was denied.'

I sat down, as I suddenly felt hot. I felt angry, very angry. I had been told that I was entitled to his date of birth. Here were human beings playing God wth my life! Well, I said to myself, that was not going to be! I would not allow it to happen. I needed to find my father, whether my father was agreeable to this, or not!

I wanted to get on with my life. I was going round in circles, wasn't anyone going to give way, and bend the rules a bit?

I knew that I wouldn't give up now, till I dropped dead of old age. I would face my father head on. He made me, he and my mother. It takes two. It's about time that the people representing the Veterans thought about that issue.

It had crossed my mind that maybe the Veterans had actually contacted my father and had a negative response. Maybe he was burying his head in the sand? Well, this was one problem daughter that was never going to go away.

Time and again I thought that maybe he was worried about his wife and family. Well I did not want to hurt them at all. There were ways that we could communicate, ways that they could never find out. We could get around it somehow.

I felt so angry, that I immediately dialled Mr Pelligrini's number. Once I was through I lasped into frantic dialogue, explaining the V.A.'s refusal to help me.

"Leave it to me Mrs Clarke, and I'll look into it."

Five days later, lying on the front door mat, was the letter that sealed my fate! My heart went into my mouth, as I realised that it was from Charles Pelligrini. He wrote, 'In response to your request for further information on L. H. McCloud, a member of the armed forces. I have been able to secure three other items of information about Mr McCloud, service number, 39721917.' My stomach turned over.

'I have discovered that his middle name is Harvey, and his birth date is December 25th 1920! My heart was pounding, and tears filled my eyes. His birthday was on Christmas Day! So if this were my father, then mum must have thought about him every Christmas day! When I thought back, she always seemed to have a wistful look on her face. The third item was, 'He entered Military Service in January 1944.'

Once more I stared at the letter. This is it! I said excitedly to myself. I sprang up from the chair, and danced a jig around the dog—to her amazement! I've got it! "Whoopee!" I shouted.

Some time later, after I had calmed down, I thought about Charles Pelligrini. I knew that I owed him a lot. I hope that I get to meet him someday, I said to myself.

I sat down. What can I do to get this man's address? I was almost there, at the top of my mountain. What would I find when I reached the summit? The reality was slowly sinking in. Questions went round and round once more. What if, when we met, we didn't like each other? Fear swept over me, I began to feel really afraid, but I knew that I would have to keep pushing till the very end!

CHAPTER 13

Soon after this I was invited along with some other War 'babes', to meet a Philip Grinton at Pamela's house. Philip was a retired Lieutenant Colonel with the U.S. corps of engineers and, interested in genealogy, has been a keen 'helper' of G.I. children searching for their fathers. Philip lived in California and was in England for a visit. It was thought to be a good idea if he met some of us, and talked to us about our searches. At the time I had this deep feeling that it would not be very long before I found my father, but I still felt that Philip might be able to give me some good advice.

The sun was shining brightly that day, as I excitedly boarded the train to Surbiton.

Later, optimism swept over me as we all sat and chatted in the secluded garden. It was my first meeting with Barbara Cowin and Anita Verender, both still searching at that time for their fathers. Sadly, the future held for them both a profound sadness, as both were to find their fathers had died.

Back in the garden we all talked in turn with Philip, and it was decided that he would try to get this L. H. McCloud's birth certificate. If his mother's name had been 'Jean', then we would know definitely that this was the man I was searching for.

The day came to an end, but little did I know that the next time I would meet Philip, would be on his home ground of California!

I saw a vision of my pathway ahead, and it looked exciting and adventurous, and yet, I felt like I was on an emotional roller coaster as my husband and I decided to part. I felt that we had grown so far apart, and wanted such different things in our lives. I had tried very hard to continue with my marriage, seeking help through 'Relate' (the old 'Marriage Guidance') and also Alanon, for families of people who had a drink problem. In the end I decided, after twenty-six years, that I would no longer make sacrifices for myself or the children, that it would be better for us to part.

I continued to push on with my search, channelling my sadness into an energy, as I had never done before.

I sat down one day, and decided to take stock of the situation. When I first found out about my father, all I had was the name of Larry. I seemed to have travelled a long way, metaphorically speaking. I said to myself that I was almost in reach of him, and yet I seemed to be stretching out my arms and not quite getting there! All the way through I had come up against brick walls, then I would push my way through them and continue on. I spent all that day thinking of how to obtain his address.

I thought about all my letters sitting in a box upstairs. Why don't I go back through these, maybe there would be something I'd forgotten that I might try again? In desperation I wearily climbed the stairs, and soon I was leafing through all the papers that I had collected over the years, when suddenly my eyes fell on a letter from Gayle B. the agency that had helped me before, in sending me that man in Georgia.

A slow smile spread across my face. That's it, I thought, I'll try her again. I know it will cost me more money, but what does that matter, if it gets me what I want in the end? I leafed through a few more papers, and came across Virgil Thompson's address as well. I immediately decided to try both of them again.

I posted my letters off and set about preparing for Christmas once more. In November I had a reply from Virgil, who had enclosed two more addresses of L. McClouds for me to try. Once more my hopes rose, but that was short lived, as I never had a reply from either of them.

If I were to meet my father, I prayed that I would resemble him in some way. That there wasn't any mistake. I knew that some people didn't have any likeness to a parent at all. What if I was like that? Anxiously I turned my hands over, studying their shape, I glanced down at my feet, and wondered if they were like his? I looked in the mirror, turning my face to one side to study my ears. I looked at my nose, and knew that I did look very much like my mother, but there must be some resemblance to him, and I hoped that it would be noticeable when I eventually stood face to face with my father.

Two weeks later I received a reply from the Gayle B. Agency. She wrote, 'There are several new sources available to me that were not available in 1989. I also have another source, if we can get a birth date.' I've got that I thought excitedly!

'It would be helpful if we could have Lawrence's middle name.' My stomach turned over.

'I'm assuming that you mean Kansas, Missouri? We also have a driver's licence check, and many people drive in their 70's; he will be 72 now. I have not been taking out of country cases for many years now, but I will try one for you. I have access to the national death register and Lawrence is not on it.'

I felt stunned. I warmed to the familar tone of her letter, it had given me so much hope of eventually getting his address. Gayle had also taken the trouble to work out this man's age, and even checked the death register for me. I never knew that there was such a thing as a 'death register'? she said it would cost sixty dollars, and so I grabbed my pen and worked it out to around forty five pounds. I felt a pang of guilt, Christmas was looming, but I knew that I would have to find the extra money somehow. The next day, I went into town and ordered an international cheque for sixty dollars, and hurriedly posted it off! Now it would be back to waiting again, but I had plenty to do for Christmas to take my mind off it!

Harold wrote towards the end of November, he had tried to telephone yet another McCloud, but with no luck. He's still trying hard, still determined that I will find my father, I thought.

My aunt June wrote, with the idea of photocopying my uncle Carl's discharge papers. I thought what a good idea. Why hadn't we thought of that before? The next week the copy of the old discharge papers plopped onto the mat. I hurried to open the envelope, removing them carefully, eager to witness another piece of history to do with World War Two. Laying the papers out on the table, I smiled as I noticed that my uncle's job had been that of repairing all types of military powered vehicles. I felt a pang as I envisioned my father underneath a huge tank, covered in grease, this was a very important job in the U.S. Army, I thought.

I noticed with interest that Carl's job before the War was controlling the mechanical doors to a coal mine. Then I felt sad, as I suddenly remembered that he had eventually died of emphysemia, a lung condition, generally brought on by coal dust.

I thought that my father had probably worked at the same job as my uncle, I wondered if I would ever know what he actually did during those grim days of the War. I knew that I was so very near to locating my father, would I be able to overcome the last hurdle and attain his address? I broke out in a sweat, feeling desperate. What if I tried and tried to get it, but never did? I felt out of control, helpless, not knowing what to do.

I began to fantasize about having loads of money and employing a private detective. He would soon 'root' out my father, like a mole burrowing away. He would soon find him. My friends had threatened to write to Cilla Black's 'Surprise, Surprise' show on the television. I began to imagine what would happen, as I sat unknowingly in the audience. Unexpectedly the spotlight would be on me as my name came over the microphone loud and clear! What if my step-father saw it. The fear of him was still with me. What would my mother have thought, as I was still so connected to her. I sighed, reality took over and I realised that I'd never have the chance to be chosen anyway.

I picked up my 'searching for a buddie' magazine and noticed an advert for World Wide Tracers. This looks interesting, if the worst comes to the worst maybe they could find out the address that I so desperately wanted! Well, I could find out their charges. A couple of weeks later, I was in receipt of their brochure and realised that at their prices, to hire a detective was way out of my reach.

I felt glad when Christmas 1992 was over, and relieved as the New Year came in. On January the 19th the all important letter that I had so eagerly been waiting for arrived. I had been keeping a careful watch for the postman, and yet when the letter came from the Gayle B. Agency, it took me completely by surprise!

I picked up the envelope and stared at it, suddenly realising that it was indeed from her. I wonder if she's had any luck? I thought, as my stomach turned over. I took a deep breath and sat down at the table, trying to keep calm in case of disappointment. I gently eased the letter out of the envelope, not really wanting to look at its contents. I slowly unfolded the paper, and read, 'Good news!' My heart did a triple somersault! I was beaming.

'The drivers licence came back and we were able to find a listing for Lawrence McCloud. My mouth dropped open, as I took a sharp intake of breath!

'Date of birth, 12-25-20. His address is ...' and continued with his address. 'The town is Weaverville.' I stared hard at the letter, this town is in California. That can't be right, I thought. Oh, no, it must be the wrong man, surely? Don't say he was in California all the time? I don't believe it! I took a deep breath.

My mind was in turmoil, I tried to stay calm as I continued to read her letter. 'I called directory assistance, but there was no phone listed for him. This is not unusual, many Californians have unlisted phone numbers. Weaverville is a small community (2,000) population. It is located in the far North section of California, probably 50 miles from the Pacific coastline? My hands shook, no wonder I couldn't find him in Kansas. Harold was right when he said, "This guy ain't here!"

I didn't know what to do first. I felt a scream rise up in my throat. I read the letter through twice more, before I could absorb its importance!

Could this really be the man that I had searched for all these years? Tears filled my eyes.

Instead of not knowing what to do next, I was faced with the powerful emotion of rejection! It was something that had always been there, lurking in the back of my mind. However if this were my father I was going to have to face it head on!

My stomach was quivering, and I felt in no fit state for work, but I grabbed my coat and my son and excitedly hurried out!

All day at work I could think of nothing else! I kept trying to calm myself down, but then I realised that I had no idea where

Weaverville actually was, and I hadn't even looked at the map. I felt an urgency then to get home as quickly as possible!

I rushed through the front door, and grabbed my map of the USA. Getting down on my knees, I unfolded the map and spread it over the grey carpet. I picked up Gayle's letter, thinking, now where did she say it was? I found on the letter the name of Weaverville, and turned my attention back to my map on the floor. I began scanning the Pacific coastline, placing my finger along it. I traced the coastline until my finger came upon a place, which I could not believe, was actually called Eureka. My mouth dropped open, didn't Galileo, the famous scientist, shout EUREKA, meaning I HAVE FOUND IT! I felt really strange, as if someone or something was trying to tell me something. It seemed almost spooky, uncanny! I continued to scrutinise the map, when suddenly my eyes rested on a river, just inland of the Pacific coastline. I peered closer, trying to fathom out the name. I took a sharp breath, as I read, *the McCLOUD river.* Right beside it was the town of Weaverville! I stared and stared, hardly daring to believe my eyes. I knew then, that no matter what happened, I was at the end of my search. I felt so excited, but then a tiny doubt crept into my mind. What if, after all these clues, it wasn't him? But this time was different, I told myself. I had nowhere else to go. I was now at Lawrence McCloud, the one who went back to the States in March 1946. The one who I had searched for in Kansas, and this man was there at the beginning of the War. There was nowhere else for me to go. I was at the top of my mountain, I just hoped I wasn't about to fall off.

After my great excitement of finding Weaverville on the map, I now had to think about my next move. It was a pity that this man didn't have a telephone number. I'm sure that my friend Harold would have gladly phoned on my behalf.

I decided to investigate for myself from England, just to be sure. I picked up the phone and dialled International Directory Enquiries, but felt disheartened as the operator confirmed the Agency's findings.

Well, now I had the address of the man I thought was my father. I knew that I was going to have to write to this man, and my stomach went over at the thought of it. I'd been through all this before, first with that man in Kansas and then stuck for a whole year with that man in Georgia, who turned out to be black! I prayed that this man would reply quickly; I didn't want to have to go through all that again!

With the children tucked up in bed, and the T.V. switched off, there would be no distractions from this all important letter. I thought about the children, how excited they would be if they were to have a nice, kind grandfather. They had known that I had been searching all these years, and I knew because of their own adoption, that they too, would probably search for biological parents. I comforted myself that at least I would really understand their need to do this.

I had kept my search 'low key', not saying too much to the children. I didn't want to get them too excited about the prospect of an 'American grampa' for fear of them being hurt by rejection if my father were to reject me.

I sat quietly on the settee, my pad and pen poised ready for my first letter that I was to compose to my father. I just couldn't get the wording to sound right, and made several attempts, until I was finally satisfied with it. I knew that I had to be diplomatic, wording my letter so carefully in case his wife opened it. I didn't want to hurt her in anyway.

After I had finished writing, I withdrew my photo album from the drawer, and carefully picked a photograph of myself and the children together. I hoped once again, that I resembled him, my biological father. Then I placed the photo with the letter, and an International reply coupon altogether in an envelope. I had written details about myself and my mother, along with what little bit of history I knew about my American family. With this information I envisioned this man would realise that I was actually his daughter.

Rejection was uppermost in my mind all the time. I would think deeply about my own expectations from my father and his family. I would say to myself over and over, all I want is a photograph and the family history, but if he did not accept me, I knew that it was not anything to do with me as a person, only the circumstances of my birth. If he did not want to meet me, then he had missed out on a wonderful daughter and two lovely grandchildren, with heaps of love to give.

I posted the letter the next morning, and began the wait, the wait that I hoped would change my life. I consoled myself, that at least I could stop this incessant searching, and get on with my own life.

I had written to my respective 'helpers' informing them of my breakthrough. I suddenly had a 'brainwave': why didn't I write to the Gayle B. Agency and ask if she would send a registered letter to L. H. McCloud, in Weaverville. I was worried that Mr McCloud might not receive my letter. What if his wife opened all the mail? At least a registered letter would have to be signed for, by Mr McCloud himself. That way I would be really sure that he got my letter. I thought that this was a really good idea and wrote a hurried note to Gayle, crossing my fingers that she would agree.

I had this terrible fear that I might be 'stuck' for another year, and I'd made up my mind, that this was most definitely not going to happen again!

It was February 1993. I was still waiting nervously for a

reply from this man. I felt anxious, out of control of the situation. I couldn't make him reply if he didn't want to, could I? Really I knew that it was early days yet, why should I feel so worried. Maybe this man had a mental illness—thoughts of Alzeimer's disease came into my mind—and wouldn't be able to answer my letters. I felt impatient waiting for the Agency's response to my request, and felt greatly relieved when she agreed to send a registered letter to Lawrence McCloud, in Weaverville. I felt a wave of gratitude. Gayle only wanted two dollars, so along with another letter for Mr McCloud, I placed it into an envelope and expectantly sent it off. I hoped that writing to this man again, who I strongly suspected was my father, might touch on his emotions. After all, I said to myself, he and my mother must have felt a strong passion for each other, a passion that some people might not experience in a whole lifetime.

So far, I had written three letters to him. If this man should choose never to reply, what could I do about it? I knew, within myself, that if he never acknowledged me, then I would go to this place called Weaverville, and at least walk straight by him. I would have to see his face. I would be comforted to know, for the rest of my life, that I had seen my father in the flesh, if only briefly. I would live with that I said to myself.

Finally, I had Gayle's letter in my hand. I felt a little apprehensive as I ripped the envelope open and removed from it a small green card. I frowned for a second, until I realised that it was a receipt, via the American mail, for my registered letter. I grinned and felt elated! This man had my letter, now I know that he really has received it!

I began tracing my finger over his signature. I could see that it was bold and strong, so to me he wasn't ill or mentally disabled. Someone who was sick or not mentally able, would have fragile writing, perhaps a spidery scrawl. Maybe they would not be able to sign their signature at all.

It was now April 1993. I had received two letters from Philip Grinton. He wrote telling me that he had requested two birth certificates, in two different states. He also added that someone from the Births/Deaths had phoned him, and asked who was actually asking for them. He had replied that is was his daughter in England.

I felt a warmth go through me, as I repeated aloud, "From his daughter in England!" And grinned.

As soon as I opened my eyes each morning, my first thoughts would be of the town of Weaverville and Mr McCloud. Perhaps this would be the day that I got a letter from him? I hoped desperately that it would be a letter of acceptance and not rejection. That he would want to know me, want to meet me. I knew that it would be hard for someone to understand. I had wondered often myself, whether it would be feasable to have a father/daughter relationship after so many years apart. Maybe that would be hard to understand, if you have a father in your life, but for me there was this curiosity. What must it feel like to have a father? It was as simple as that.

Every morning, as I sleepily came downstairs, my whole self was drawn to the front door wondering about the postman. Has he been? When nothing arrived, my heart would sink, and a feeling of gloom would waft over me.

Thoughts of this man were consuming me. I seemed to be functioning on auto pilot. I wanted to know one way or another, it was so frustrating!

I began to prepare myself for the worst. I had read in TRACE'S newsletters of the sad stories of G.I. fathers refusing to meet their offspring. A feeling of deep anger would come over me, after all they had helped to make their children. Maybe I was being unfair, but I thought, they had the pleasure, while the woman was left to bear the pain. Those men who refused to meet their children were cowards as far as I was concerned!

One evening, a few weeks later, I sat quietly, when suddenly I thought, I will write L. H. McCloud one more letter. It would be the final one. My stomach was in knots, as I knew deep down that this was my biological father, and this was the end of the road, as far as I was concerned. At the same time, as I sat deep in thought, it came to me, why don't I write to a social worker in Weaverville as well. There was no way that I could allow things to drag on and on, so I made the decision there and then, that writing to a social worker as well, was the best idea.

As I began composing my letter, I started to grasp that it was beginning to sound rather curt, and abrupt. My impatience was showing in my writing, compared to the polite letters of the past. At one point in the letter, I wrote that I felt it was extremely rude not to answer my correspondence. Finally when I had completed both letters, I felt drained. It had taken all my emotions to almost 'imprint' myself on to the pages, of what was to be my final letter to my G.I. soldier father. Relief flooded over me as I licked the enevelope and stamp, ready for posting and went to bed.

It was May 19th. I had a letter from the Department of Health in Kansas. The letter informed me that there was no birth certificate for Lawrence McCloud. I felt a twinge of confusion. He must have been born somewhere else, I thought. I took a deep breath, letting these feelings go, as I knew it was just a matter of time.

CHAPTER 15

It was May 23rd, around midnight. I'd had a late night, and as I crawled into bed, I immediately fell into a deep sleep.

Somewhere in the far distance, I could hear a telephone ringing. I sat up quickly, suddenly realising that it was my phone, and not a dream. Anxiously, I swung my legs over the side of the bed, and stumbled half-asleep down the stairs! Almost at the bottom of the stairs was a stair-gate, used as a 'dog stopper'. Slightly agitated, I grabbed the banister and clambered over it! Breathlessly, I grabbed the phone thinking of the children who would wake and never go to sleep again. My son, especially, with his boundless energy, like a battery with such a long life that it NEVER ran down!

I tried to catch my breath, as I said, "Hello?" puzzled as to who on earth it could be at this time of the night.

"Is that Norma Jean Clarke?" It was a man with a soft American accent.

"Yes," I said, still half-asleep.

"Your mother's name was Edna ... ?"

"Yes?" How does he know my mother's name, I thought?

"Have you been searching for your father, Lawrence McCloud?" Excitement rose in his voice.

"Yes!" By this time my mind was racing. I couldn't make sense of what this man actually wanted!

"Well," he paused. "This is your half-brother, Peter McCloud!"

I gasped, "Oh, my God!" And fell down onto my knees!

The hair stood up on the back of my neck, and I became aware of goose pimples all over my body! For a second I couldn't speak, my mouth dropped open and I let out a cry! I felt stunned!

"I don't believe it," I managed to blurt out. "I must be dreaming!" My new brother laughed!

I was still stunned, and warmed to his American voice, as total unreality wafted over me.

"Our father has asked me to phone you, Norma Jean." The tears trickled slowly down my cheeks.

"He hasn't got a telephone, so he asked me to call you. He told me to give you a message." I wiped my eyes with the back of my hand.

"He is so ashamed that he didn't answer your letters, but he didn't know how to tell his other children." I felt a pang, understanding at last, why he hadn't replied.

I answered, "I'm really sorry that I put him in that situation, but there was nothing else that I could do." For a second I felt guilty, but soon let that go.

I've got a brother. All my life I'd wished for a brother, now I had one!

I could hear the excitement in Peter as he said, "You have another half-brother, Harvey!" I gasped again.

"He lives in Kansas, and is doing a Philosophy degree at the University there. He's two years older than you." I was beaming as I thought, how funny that I should like philosophy too!

"You have a younger sister, Mary, and she has six children!" He said laughingly.

"Six children!" I exclaimed! How funny that we should both

have a love of children.

"She also has nineteen cats!" He laughed again.

"Nineteen cats!" I repeated after him, suddenly visualising felines roaming everywhere!

"People keep turning up with them, and she hasn't the heart to turn them away!" He laughed again.

I could feel the emotion rising in me, at the realisation that I had finally made contact with my father!

Peter then went on to tell me that he was 35 years old and Mary was a year younger. As he was telling me all this I stretched out my hand and reached for the note pad at the side of the phone. I then grabbed the pen and began scribbling down all the information that he had been telling me.

Peter went on talking, "Dad says to tell you to come over as soon as you can. He lives alone in a big house, he has plenty of room."

Tears pricked at my eyes again, as I thought that this was really more than I could hope for.

"Oh, Peter, I'd love to, but I would have to try to raise the money somehow." I felt doubts as to how on earth I would be able to do this.

"Dad says, that although he's not a big letter writer, he'll be writing soon." My new brother was as excited as I was, I could tell, and he was talking to me as if we'd known each other all our lives. I felt a mixture of sadness and happiness at that thought.

"Look I'm going to write to you tonight with all the family history, and I'll try to find a suitable photo," he said softly.

I was having feelings of panic, as I realised we were going to have to say goodbye.

I was still frantically jotting down notes, I didn't want to forget anything that Peter told me.

Suddenly, he said,

"Our Great grandmother was a full-bloodied Mohawk Indian, and our Great grandfather came from the Isle of Skye, in Scotland, England!" I felt stunned, my mother had said that there was an Indian in the family! How proud I felt, to be a part of such a heritage. It somehow felt just right to me!

I hastily jotted down 'Mohawk' in case I forgot the name of my ancestral tribe that I had unknowingly been a descendant of since birth.

"I'm going to have to go, Norma Jean," his voice lowered, as he spoke.

I loved him calling me Norma Jean, and felt I would use it a lot more in the future, as it sounded like the American-half of me!

"I don't want to say goodbye to you, Peter. I really don't believe that this phone call has happened!" A sob rose up in my throat.

"Bye, Norma Jean." His voice cracked.

"Bye Peter, don't forget to write."

I put the phone down, and slowly rose up from the floor, and putting my head in my hands I began to cry. In the silence of the night, I stood still, bewildered. Suddenly the reality of what had just happened overtook me, and I had this sudden impulse to fling the front door wide open, and run out into the street yelling my news to everyone!

The quietness of the house reminded me that it was past midnight, and most people that lived down the street, would be fast asleep! Instead, I turned, my stomach churning, and walked back towards the stairs. I wanted so desperately to tell someone, but it was so late. Shall I wake the children? I thought, but decided against it, as sleep would be impossible for the rest of the night.

I climbed back slowly up the stairs, still feeling a kind of numbness as I crawled back into bed. I doubted if I would be able to sleep. I lay wide eyed, reliving the conversation I'd just had with my new found brother, Peter.

It was all so hard to take in. After all those years of searching, I had now found two new brothers and a sister. I felt sad that we had not played together as children, but that's how it was, there was nothing we could do to change that.

I suddenly thought of all those nephews and nieces I now had. I hoped to meet them sometime. As I lay there in the darkness, I thought of my father and wondered what he looked like. I wonder if he's tall or fat! I knew that I would have to get to meet him as quickly as possible. But how? I don't have any money. I could only see one way and that was with something that I had always dreaded — publicity.

I thought about my brother, Peter. How strange that he should have the same name as my estranged husband, and my aunt Jill's husband was called Peter too. The connection seemed uncanny!

I suddenly thought of my stepfather finding out, and my stomach tightened with thoughts of my childhood once more. It seems ridiculous to me now, but I thought there had been enough pain for all of us already.

Often when thinking about my actions then, I believe it was feelings arising from my childhood, that influenced me in that way.

It was no good, I said to myself, I would have to get publicity, but maybe I could just go for American publicity. I might get away with it.

I felt so excited at the prospect of meeting my father, but it had to be soon. I knew that I wouldn't be able to get it out of my mind, then I thought, what if something happened to my father, or happened to me? I felt an urgency, I've got to get there as quickly as possible. I would never get over it, if after all the years of searching, something drastic happened, that stopped us from meeting.

Finally my eyes grew heavy, and I drifted off into a fitful sleep.

The next morning, when I awoke, I suddenly opened my eyes wide with a start! I felt a warmth in my toes, and I began to smile to myself. The phone call, that amazing phone call from my new American brother, Peter! I sat bolt upright in bed! I've found my father, I thought, excitedly! Then doubts began to creep into my mind. Did that telephone call really happen? Was it really just a dream? I jumped out of bed, grabbed my dressing gown, and ran down the stairs. I knew where the proof of my astounding phone call lay. I dashed to the telephone, and picked up the pad, breathing a sigh of relief as I read my hurriedly scrawled notes, written the night before. I rushed into the front room, and blurted out my news to the amazement of the children! I had this urge to dance around the room, much to their embarrassment!

All the rest of that day I seemed to be floating on air. I was bursting to tell everyone my good news! I dashed through the double doors of my workplace, to comments, "you look like you've won the pools!"

That day, I began to realise, was my first day of being a complete person. I knew my origins, I knew who I was at last!

My long suffering friends were almost as excited as I was, being so patient with me over the years. Now, they could look forward to a rest from me and my long search for my father. My self-worth had slowly and steadily been building up over the years, now I was up on my 'pedestal'. I knew that I had changed beyond recognition! I began to think positively about the best time to try to go to California. It was May, and I decided that the summer holidays would be best.

During my conversation with Peter, he had said that his mother was deceased. I thought about my father's wife, and how sad he must have been at her loss, remembering my own mother's death. Again, I wondered, and hoped that I had some resemblance to my father, even in the slightest way. Well, it wouldn't be long before this was going to happen, and I would be able to gaze at his face and witness this for myself.

I wondered if my father was lonely, as he lived alone. I thought of my mother's words 'he was a very kind man.' Those words had been imprinted on my mind, and with these thoughts of my father, I felt that we would get along, that we would like each other. I began to wonder if he might be artistic. I had always wondered where I got my love of art from. I knew it wasn't from my mother, maybe I'd inherited it from him.

That day, after work, I rushed to open out my map again. I had this really strong need to look for Weaverville once more, imagining my father there, as I gazed at it. I searched for San Francisco, I knew that we would have to fly there. Well, we wouldn't be flying anywhere if I couldn't raise the money, I said to myself. But I knew that I would not let it beat me.

CHAPTER 16

As promised, my new brother, Peter, sent me a letter straight after our exciting phone call.

I couldn't contain myself as I tore open the envelope, and began to read. His letter cemented the fact that I had made contact with him as I read the history of my American family. In the letter Peter told me that our American grandmother's name was actually Lois, but thought that perhaps she was called Jean, he didn't know her middle name, but that was probably how my mother came to give me the middle name of Jean. Sadly she had died in 1981, and I had not even been aware of her existence.

Peter had included so many interesting facts about my grandmother and how she had diabetes, writing that 'these were important traits that I should know about'. He also wrote about our father's war-time experiences in Europe, and their idyllic childhood in Weaverville.

I read and re-read his letter, later putting it carefully away with all my other precious letters.

Once again I waited eagerly for the postman, for the all important letter from my father. I sighed, would he really write to me. I couldn't bring myself to believe it. I braced myself for disappointment.

Early one morning, as we rushed around getting ready for

school and work, my son rushed in waving a brown envelope in the air!

"Mum, it's from America, can I open it?" He said breathlessly.

I saw the disappointment in his eyes as I said, "Sorry, Adam, but this is one letter that MUM is going to open!"

At first I studied the envelope, savouring the moment. My father's handwriting looked strong and clear, and I ran my fingers over it. Then very quickly I began to open it. I thought, there must be a photo in here, and felt anxious, as I thought, what if I don't like the look of him? My hands shook, as I gently removed the contents, and my eyes fell on the photo that he had enclosed. I looked wistfully at it, first noticing that he looked fairly tall. I could see that he had a small moustache, but as soon as I looked at his face, I knew for certain then, that he was my biological father. It was something in his bone structure, the shape of his face, I could see it was the same as mine! How funny, I thought, this man has been walking around in America, looking like me. I liked him immediately.

I slowly unfolded his letter, and with my heart fluttering, began to read,

'Dear Norma Jean,

I'm so sorry for taking so long to answer your letters, but I have been so shocked. I just didn't know how to handle this. I am a widower, and have been since Dec.1991. I have three children, two boys and one girl. (I immediately thought: No, two girls!) *I have 11 grandchildren.* (I thought: No, 13!)

So I finally got up the courage to tell the others about you and they really couldn't believe it! But truly they seemed to take it pretty good, and accepted the idea that they have a new sister.'

My father went on to recall how he met my mother. *'I wasn't stationed at Stansted, I was stationed in France!'* Stationed in France? Oh, no, I'd looked for all those years in the wrong place! His letter continued, confirming what my mother had said to me, that he'd had a letter from her suspecting that she was pregnant. He replied to her, but never heard from her again.

'Well, Norma-Jean,' he wrote, *'you don't have to search any more for your dad. I would be right proud if you would call me Dad.'* A tear trickled slowly down my face. *'You are my daughter and I'm proud to know you.'* Then he wrote a P.S. at the bottom, which made me feel warm inside. *'I forgot to tell you, you are beautiful in your photo. Love, Dad.'*

The tears flowed freely, then. This must be what it feels like to have a father, I thought to myself.

I read that letter over and over, and I knew that I must get to California, somehow.

That day I decided to phone my friend Reg Robinson (the researcher at Stansted) and tell him the good news! I began to tell him about my need for publicity, when suddenly he said, "Leave that to me, Norma. I have a friend who works in London for the N.B.C.(American TV.) In fact he owes me a favour."

I was speechless, not expecting my publicity to come through Reg, at the same time my stomach went over. The thought that I would be letting the 'cat out of the bag', with regard to my stepfather, was very worrying. I knew that my childhood programming was still with me, but now, this was for me, I had to get to America somehow.

I poured myself a cup of tea, and with my mind racing, I sank into the armchair. A part of me was on a high, but the other part was emotionally drained, although I knew that I would never have peace of mind until I had done this.

Mal Redding, the NBC reporter phoned straight away, and an agreement was very quickly reached for the show's producer, Lynne Edwards, and himself to visit me the next day. I felt bewildered and slightly niggled at the speed they worked. I felt anxious, and thought my mother would not like this. But I quickly brushed those thoughts away, replacing them with the thought that this was *my* life, this was for *me!*

After their arrival the next day, we sat chatting about my story, and Mal said, "Well, Norma, this is what we are offering you. We would like you to come into our studios in London, and link up live with breakfast T.V. in New York."

I stared at him, feeling shocked!

"Then we would fly your father to New York, and he would speak to you via the satellite." He smiled at me.

I took a deep breath, this wasn't happening to me, was it? I had this sudden vision of being besieged by camera men. I would come downstairs one morning, swishing open the curtains, and to my surprise I would witness cameramen crouching in the bushes, just outside my home, trying their hardest to snatch a photograph of me!

Mal could see I was struck dumb, so he continued, "Then after that we would fly you and your children to New York, where you would meet your father for the very first time." He paused, waiting for my answer.

I felt nervous. I didn't much like the idea of meeting my father so publicly, but I also knew that I couldn't afford the fare, either. What shall I do, I thought frantically!

"I don't believe it!" Was all I could manage to say.

I felt as if I were in a dream, and visualized our first meeting. What would I say to him? My stomach turned over. Would we laugh? Would we cry? Would I feel the same way as I did when I met a stranger? Yet, was he really a stranger? After all I had been walking around with one half of his genes all my life!

I suddenly realised something, "How will we get in touch with my father, he hasn't got a telephone."

"That's a thought!" Mal replied.

I had my new brother, Peter's, telephone number, but he worked shifts in a hospital, and lived at least an hour away from our father.

We discussed the time difference, and began to realise that it wasn't going to be easy fixing this important rendezvous. I had no idea what my father would think. I had no idea what sort of person he was. Somehow, I felt that he was a fairly private person, as he had said that it was quite a shock, and hard for him to take in.

A week had gone by, and I hadn't heard from the NBC. I felt agitated and out of control, not knowing what was going on. I didn't want to say too much to the children, in case we were let down. Finally I couldn't bear the suspense any longer, and picked up the phone and rang the NBC.

"We're having difficulty contacting Peter, it's always his answer phone."

I decided to ring Peter, and put a message on the machine, myself. So I took a deep breath, and asked Peter to telephone me. Later that same evening, I spoke for the second time to my new brother.

After explaining everything to him, it was agreed that he would travel to Weaverville to see our father the following Thursday, his day off.

Waiting for the results of his visit was nerve racking. All the plans that we had hoped for seemed imminent, and yet on hold. I had talked myself round to looking forward to it, and I now knew that I was going to be very disappointed if it was all called off. I had thought about warning my aunt June, in Florida, to watch out for her breakfast T.V., but decided against that idea, as my sixth sense was preparing me for a let down!

Finally the producer of NBC telephoned. "Well, Norma-Jean, it looks like your father does not want to do this."

I let out a sigh.

"Your brother has been to visit him twice now, and he'd rather not do it."

I had been preparing myself for this, and could really understand his reluctance. After all, to fly all that way to New York, to meet me in front of millions of people, could not be easy.

My heart was heavy, as I replaced the receiver. With shoulders hunched, I walked back slowly into the lounge. I felt so deflated, after finding the publicity I wanted, now I had to think of another way to go.

By this time, my father and I had written to each other again. To put him at ease, I wrote, 'it'll be alright Dad when we meet.'

I knew that my fathers generation, who had fought in a war, known deprivation as we never would, did not accept 'out of wedlock' children, as we so readily did.

I didn't have a plan. What could I do? Why did I think that it would come easy? I always did things the hard way, but at least I was strong.

The telephone rang a week later.

"Hello, is that Norma Jean Clarke?" A young woman's voice. "We have been given your name and phone number. You are hoping to meet your father for the first time?" She sounded pleasant.

"Well, I hope so, by this summer." I felt puzzled.

She went on, "We are a film company who are making a film on the whole aspect of World War Two, and the G.I.'s are a part of it." My stomach lurched. Here we go again.

"We would like to film you at home, and then to travel with

you to meet your father."

I gripped the telephone tighter, excitement rising in me.

My mind was reeling, how would I know if my father would agree to this? It was so difficult. If only I could actually speak to him.

She spoke again, "We would take you right to your father's front door."

Right to my father's front door! That would be marvellous! I had thought about the daunting journey, travelling alone with the children.

"When would this be shown on British T.V?" Thoughts of my stepfather loomed.

"It wouldn't be shown till June 1994," she replied.

It didn't take me long to make up my mind. How else could I get to meet my father? I reasoned.

I quickly wrote off to him, explaining to him the situation, and would he mind this? Before long, and with great excitement, I had his letter of consent.

I phoned the TV. company, and explained that I needed to go in the summer. Mostly, because of my anxiety about anything happening to my father or to me before we met, but also because it was holiday time for the children and myself. After speaking to them on the phone, I sighed, and began the wait for things to be discussed and put into motion. I hoped that they would give me a date fairly soon, so that I could make preparations myself.

I was beginning to get quite excited, but with reservations. I knew that I was somewhat naive and trusting, not knowing anything about the legal procedures of making a film. I believed that the company would keep their word. After all, I knew what a fantastic story we had.

It was now July 1993. I had checked the last date that we

could fly out to San Francisco, and be back in time for the new school term. I hadn't heard anything from the film company, and was feeling edgy. I decided to phone the researcher. I felt satisfied as she explained about meetings with the airline involved, and still trusted their word.

Time was going by. I felt so frustrated as I had so many preparations to make. I felt uneasy, and as before, I felt totally out of control. All my life I'd had to take care of myself, and here I was, out of control with the most important thing in my life—going to meet my father.

Did these people not realise how important a meeting this was? I had searched for almost seven years, it had taken up so much of my life. Was it so unreasonable to want to meet my father as soon as possible? Why couldn't the film company understand that? I phoned the film company again.

"I need to know if you are going to film me meeting my father," I need a definite yes or no!" I said in desperation.

The researcher replied, "They are still trying to get the go-ahead from the airlines?" My heart sank. I somehow felt that she was trying to 'fob' me off.

"Look I need a definite yes!" I was feeling angry now, as she placed her hand over the mouthpiece. I could hear muffled tones as she spoke to someone.

"The producer is saying, can you do it in September?"

"Oh, that's it, ask me for September and then it will be October?" I heard my voice rising.

She said suddenly, "The producer is saying, it's a definite YES!" I breathed a sigh of relief, and immediately calmed down.

"When is the very last date that you can go by?" she asked, sounding as eager as I felt now.

"By the 18th August, that will give me a few days when we

get back." I knew I was grinning.

"Right we'll be in touch soon, as soon as things are finalised.

As I put the phone down, I felt a scream rise up in my throat! We're on our way, I thought excitedly. It was now August and two weeks before my deadline. I decided to phone the researcher, although my instinct was telling me that something wasn't quite right because they would have been ringing me, wouldn't they? My heart sank as I was informed that my particular researcher was no longer there. I felt suspicious, and had a terrible 'sinking' feeling. I knew in my heart of hearts, that they were going to let me down! Eventually the producer rang me from his car.

"I'm very sorry, but can you do it next June?"

"You must be joking?" Was he trying to let me down gently?

"The people who are buying the film want to do it then." His voice faded away.

"Look." I felt really angry, with his insensitivity. "I have never met my father. It took me almost seven years to find him, what if something should happen to him, or me, between now and next June. How would he or I feel, if we'd just missed each other by a few short months? No, I'm sorry but it has to be now."

I felt sick, as we said goodbye. I knew the producer really didn't care about the emotions that were involved. A part of me knew that he had made a big mistake, missing out on our wonderful reunion. Did they not have any compassion at all? Maybe they kept me waiting to make sure that no one else got a 'scoop' from my story! I felt it was too late now to go with publicity. Well, enough is enough! I said to myself. I was back in control, and didn't need anyone's help.

I would trust no one, I'd only have faith in myself!

CHAPTER 17

After the let-down of the film company, I walked about in a daze. A lump welled up in my throat. I had already sent a postcard to my father, he would be expecting me.

Tears filled my eyes.

I still had to go, I knew that, but how on earth could I do it? I thought about an appeal to our local paper, but then my whole story would be out and I was trying to keep everything hush-hush here in England.

I decided to telephone some airlines with my story, but none of them were interested. I wrote letters to Virgin and British Airways, in desperation, just in case ...

I thought about California, knowing that CBS Television was there. Maybe they would be interested? I had a sudden thought. I found their London number and quickly dialled them, immediately lapsing into my story. The operator seemed a bit confused, and said quickly,

"I'll transfer you to Los Angeles." I opened my mouth to say something, but it was too late. I could hear the dull tone of their telephone ringing.

A very sleepy young lady answered.

"Hello, CBS News." I felt almost as surprised as she was. Desperation again in my voice as I tried to explain my need to get to California.

"There's no one here, Ma'am. It would be better if you rang

in the morning." As weary as I felt, I found myself stifling a laugh, and thought, how ridiculous! I had told her I was phoning from England, if it's her morning, then it will be my night! I quickly said goodbye, replaced the phone back on its receiver. This is not the way to go, I said to myself.

The phone rang again. "Hello, is that Norma Jean Clarke? This is a researcher for 'London Tonight' program.

She had heard about my story, and went on to invite me to the studios in London, linking live with San Francisco. For a brief second my spirits rose, but were just as quickly dashed, as I realised that I couldn't contact my father to talk to him about this. I felt hopelessness sweep over me, as I sadly turned down their offer. It was no use, I thought, as my special trip seemed to be moving further and further away from me.

My mind was in turmoil. If I say I'm going to do something, then I'm going to do it, or die in the process, I thought frantically.

I sat down, trying desperately to think of something. All of a sudden, like a bolt out of the blue, I remembered an insurance that we had decided to change on our property. Some months before, we had decided to change from an Endowment mortgage to an ordinary repayment one. I knew that these transactions take some time, and through all the trauma, I'd completely forgotten about it. I knew that all the forms had been filled in, it was really just a question of getting the money. I was angry with myself for not thinking of it sooner.

I sat down with my pad and pen, and worked out that it would be just enough for my trip!

I phoned the Building Society, no one could find it, but eventually our insurance man in Sussex, sorted it out, and said that the money would be with me sometime next week. I was beginning to panic, as there was only one week now, to my deadline. But on the strength of the insurance man's word, I decided to risk it and take the children up to Oxford Street, to buy presents for our new family.

All the time, I had this feeling that I would be buying plane tickets one day, and flying out the next! Still I thought, maybe that's the best way to go!

I thought about my father, waiting for me, how curious he must feel, waiting for this unknown English daughter? Could I really travel eight thousand miles alone, with my children? My stomach went over. When we arrived in San Francisco, I'd then got to travel on a Greyhound bus, around three hundred miles up to the mountains. I would be on 'strange' soil and yet was not America my country too?

I'd managed to keep my spirits up for so long, but I knew now that my determination to do this was flagging. I felt sad. I should be gone by next week, but I didn't even have the money. I felt really down, I had tried so hard. I just needed one last push.

Suddenly my friends seemed to sense my lethargy, and began to urge me on! They began, in a sense, to try to come with me over my final hurdle, and that was to attain the flights, then to help choose my clothes for my trip to America.

At that time I could not shake of thoughts of my stepfather. I had always thought that he was my father for forty years of my life! I knew how angry he would be about my finding my biological father. Only his feelings counted, as far as he was concerned, mine had never been considered all my life.

It was Sunday August 15th. I found it hard to believe that we would be on our way in just a few days, after all I still hadn't received the insurance money. Anxiety swept over me.

That same day the telephone rang.

"Hi, Norma Jean, how's it going?" An American voice! I

frowned, then I suddenly realised it was Philip Grinton, my 'helper' in California.

"Hello Philip, this is a surprise, how are you?"

For a second I wondered why he was ringing?

"I heard from Pamela (Winfield), the TV. company pulled out?"

"Yes, it's terrible. I've been trying to raise the money myself," I said, exasperated.

"You're going to book flights to San Francisco?"

"Well, I've thought it through, I'll have to start looking tomorrow.

"That's great, listen, give me a quick call when you've got your tickets, and I'll meet you in San Francisco!" He laughed.

I felt stunned, speechless. Tears came to my eyes.

"What, oh, how wonderful! I don't know how to thank you!" I laughed, feeling so excited!

"That's okay, I'll wait to hear from you."

"Yes, I'll phone you as soon as I have the tickets in my hand!"

I slowly replaced the receiver, and for a second stood and stared at the phone, then slowly turned and walked into the front room. How kind Philip was, I thought. What a difference it would make to us, knowing that someone was waiting for us at the other end.

I moved my finger up and wiped a tear from the corner of my eye. What was it Philip actually said? I'll meet you in San Francisco? I laughed out loud, as I imagined that it sounded just like the title of a Hollywood movie!

I began to think deeply about the enormity of this journey that I wanted to take. I was going thousands of miles from home, to stay with an elderly man I'd never met. I began to think very deeply about my journey and the man I so desperately wanted to come face to face with. What if I didn't like him? What if he drank a lot, or didn't wash? I closed my eyes and allowed my instincts to take over, they told me that everything would be alright.

I had always been a bit of an optimist, now I pulled on that optimism, as I prepared for the greatest adventure of my life!

It was now Monday, and just a few short days until I wanted to leave. I had decided to visit my bank and ask for their help. I had been informed that the insurance money would not arrive until Wednesday, that was too late as far as I was concerned. I needed to buy my tickets before then.

My friend Chris Nicholson rang.

"Well, what's happening? How are you getting your tickets?"

"I'm going to the bank first, and then I'm going to start phoning around!" I replied.

"Now, Norma, you know that I have always been a frustrated travel agent! Let me ring around for you, while you're at the bank."

I breathed a sigh of relief. I had been feeling so drained. My mind could only focus on one thing, and that was to secure the money, or we wouldn't be going anywhere.

"Oh, Chris, that would be marvellous! That would help me so much, thanks!"

Chris has as much drive, if not more, than me. She must have sensed that I needed someone to take over at that time. I looked quickly at my watch, there was half an hour before my appointment at the bank. I said a hasty goodbye to my friend, and my daughter and I went to get the car out of the garage.

Once in the car, I turned the ignition key. Click, click. Oh, no, I felt myself go hot. There's something wrong with the car. For five minutes I tried to start the engine, but I knew there was something wrong with the car that no amount of turning the ignition key, would fix.

I turned to my daughter, "Right Hayley, we'll have to walk to the bank, or we'll miss our appointment!"

One mile and half an hour later, we hurried, puffing and blowing, into the bank.

I felt really anxious, as so much hung on their compassion and whether they believed me or not.

Finally I was sitting in the office, opposite a very young lady. I felt extremely uneasy, as I thought, was this young girl going to make a decision on my life. My heart was pounding, so much rested on this!

Briefly I told this young lady my story, and that I only needed an overdraft for a few days at the most. Enough to enable me to purchase my tickets.

I looked into her face and sensed impending doom. I could tell that the decision had already been made, almost before I had crossed the threshold of the bank.

They turned me down! I was absolutely devastated. This was my last chance, my last chance to go to the U.S. within my deadline. Thoughts of my father waiting for me to arrive at that time, haunted me.

The feeling of panic returned, and I said quickly,

"Look can I use your phone please?"

I telephoned my insurance man in Sussex. He was quite annoyed, and told me to tell the bank that the cheque would be faxed to them straight away.

The overdraft was still denied, on the grounds that the cheque would not have cleared by the time I flew out of the country.

I slumped down in the chair, it was no good, the money was almost there, why would they not help me? I knew now that I would have to borrow the money, but from who or where?

In the meantime we had arrived home, and I had spoken to

my friend Chris who had held several flights for me! That was great, I thought, but I still didn't have the money.

Suddenly my backdoor opened, and standing on the threshold was uncle Les, and in his hand was his life's savings.

"Here take it until your insurance money comes through."

Tears welled up in my eyes, I felt so grateful to him that I flung my arms around his neck and kissed him! It wasn't all the amount I needed, but it was a start. I could put the rest on my Visa card, and felt eternally grateful for Les's kind gesture towards me.

It was now Tuesday. I had double checked the flights that Chris had been kind enough to hold for me, and finally chosen three that flew into San Francisco on the Thursday. With a sense of unreality, I made plans to travel into the City of London the next day, to pick up the plane tickets.

It was early evening, the phone rang. "Mrs Clarke." It was my insurance man, from Sussex.

"I'm ringing to tell you that I have faxed cash into your bank account tonight, so you'll be able to draw on it in the morning!"

I gasped! I couldn't believe that I had heard correctly, could this really be true?

Tears rolled down my cheeks, "Oh, thank God! I can't thank you enough, I don't know what to say, you've saved my life!"

I felt so happy that I didn't have to borrow the money from my uncle anymore.

The next morning, my friend, Sue Feeder, hurried round. She was going to look after Hayley and Adam, while I travelled into London to collect the flight tickets from the travel agents.

This was going to take quite some organisation, as I had to go to the bank, withdraw the cash, then go to my Building Society and get a cheque made out for the flights. Then I had to get to Oakwood tube station and travel approximately sixteen stops, then walk a mile to the travel agents to collect the tickets.

In my state of mind, which was a mixture of excitement, apprehension, tiredness and unreality, all that I had to do that morning, was daunting!

As I sat on the underground train, I felt as if I had a permanent grin on my face. I looked around at my fellow travellers, and was bursting to tell them about the amazing trip that I was about to make! Could they not see it on my face, that I was making a very special journey? I smiled to myself.

Worry overtook my happiness, as I walked the mile to the travel agents. I knew that I wouldn't feel right until I had those tickets actually in my hand. I finally arrived at the travel agents.

"I've come to collect my tickets to San Francisco for tomorrow."

I felt decidely uneasy as the travel agent searched for information on my travel documents.

"Yes, we have your flights booked." I breathed a sigh of relief. "But until you have given us your cheque, we cannot make the tickets up. This will take about two hours." My heart sank.

What could I do for two hours? I hurried out of the shop, and telephoned my friend Sue, and spoke to the children. After wandering aimlessly around for two hours, I sat and watched as the travel agent carefully placed my tickets into their wallets. At the same time, he listened amazed, as I related my story! As I talked to him it seemed as if it wasn't me that I was talking about, but someone else!

Tears came to my eyes as he finally passed the tickets over to me and I stood up to leave. I prepared myself for the long journey back home, but I was feeling much more at ease, allowing myself to get excited. Now, I really would be meeting my father at last.

Gatwick Airport, August, 1993.
Norma Jean on the way to meet her father.

1993
Norma Jean (centre), with Philip Grinton and Hayley, on the way to Anderson, C.A., to meet her father.

Norma Jean's first meeting with her 'new' brother, Peter, on a street corner in Anderson — where she almost changed her mind!

Norma Jean's treasured first photo of her father,
which he sent to her in May, 1993, with the inscription:
"To Norma Jean,
With Love—Dad"

Redding, August 1993
The first photo to be taken of Norma Jean with her father.

Redding, August 1993
Taken outside Mary's home
at Norma Jean's first meeting with her father.
(L.toR.) Peter, Norma Jean, Lawrence, Mary

Weaverville, C.A.
The home town of Norma Jean's father.

The 'quaint' old cinema in Weaverville

Norma Jean's father outside his church in Weaverville, C.A.

Norma Jean and Lawrence, her father, looking through her Search papers.

Adam and Hayley with Smokey the Bear

Norma Jean with her father at Trinity County Fair

*Norma Jean with Patricia Hicks
Journalist for the Trinity County Journal*

Norma Jeans father, Lawrence, with 'Foot' the cat.

England, December, 1993.
Norma Jean's first meeting with 'new' brother Harvey.

Norma Jean Clarke with her father, Lawrence McCloud.

NAME: McCloud, Lawrence H.

SERIAL/SERVICE NUMBERS: 39721917

DATE OF BIRTH: N/A

DATES OF SERVICE: December 28, 1943 - March 1, 1946

CITY/TOWN AND STATE OF RESIDENCE, DATE OF ADDRESS: Kansas City, Missouri
March 1, 1946

MARITAL STATUS: N/A

DEPENDENTS: N/A

RANK/GRADE: Private First Class

SALARY: N/A

ASSIGNMENTS AND THEIR GEOGRAPHICAL LOCATION: N/A

SOURCE OF COMMISSION: N/A

MILITARY AND CIVILIAN EDUCATIONAL LEVEL: N/A

PROMOTION SEQUENCE NUMBER: N/A

DECORATIONS AND AWARDS: N/A

DUTY STATUS: Discharged

PHOTOGRAPH: N/A

RECORDS OF COURTS-MARTIAL TRIALS: N/A

PLACE OF INDUCTION AND SEPARATION: Riverside, California - Jefferson Barracks, Missouri

IF VETERAN IS DECEASED: PLACE OF BIRTH:

LAST KNOWN ADDRESS:

DATE AND GEOGRAPHICAL LOCATION OF DEATH:

PLACE OF BURIAL:

* N/A denotes information not available in records

CHAPTER 18

I arrived back from the travel agents to a flurry of activity. I felt an energy and excitement coursing through me at the thought that we could pack!

One of the many, many phone calls that I had that day was from the retired Lieutenant Colonel, Philip Grinton, (my 'helper' in California).

"Hi, Norma Jean, how are you, have you managed to get the tickets, yet?" I could tell that he was as eager as I was to 'get the show on the road!'

"Yes, I've just got back, and now I can give you the flight details." My stomach went into my mouth at the thought of the long haul flight right across the USA.

After taking the details, Philip said, "Look, Norma Jean, if you like, I will meet you and the kids at the airport, and drive you to my house, where you could stay the night. Then the next day, I would be happy to drive you to meet your dad."

I took a breath,

"Oh, Philip would you? It's a long way, about three hundred miles up into the mountains." Had he really thought about the long journey? I held my breath again. Was I really talking about something that was actually going to happen? I had thumbed through the tickets, checked and double checked our flight times, but it still seemed as if it was going to happen to someone else.

I felt choked. Philip was being so kind, I just wasn't used to thoughtfulness from a man. I would never be able to repay him, ever!

Suddenly Philip replied, "Sure, it's okay. Right! I have all your details, I'll see you in San Francisco!" He laughed!

As I replaced the receiver, I thought, how lucky I am to know him.

My adrenaline was really running high now. There was so much to do. There were clothes to be washed and then packed. I didn't have any decent suitcases, but my friend, Chris Nicholson, was on her way to lend me hers.

Later, Chris bustled in, not only carrying suitcases, but shirts, 'T' shirts, shorts, and she'd even thought of a decent camera! I knew that it was going to be so important to take some good photos. Then a wave of sadness came over me, at the thought of no video film being shot of us now. I soon shrugged off those thoughts, as friends began to call round, armed with more shorts and 'T' shirts, and good luck cards! At one point, that day, I opened my front door, to find even more shorts and a pair of shoes, lying on my doorstep!

Amongst all this, my daughter still had a hundred local newspapers to deliver. I felt exasperated, as there had not been enough time to employ someone else to do it. I shrugged my shoulders, and resigned myself that we'd just have to get on with it! I suddenly found myself in the middle of packing, and yet on the other hand, breathlessly running up and down people's garden paths, frantically rolling newspapers and shoving them at top speed, into their letter boxes!

At last, that was completed and my conscience was clear. Now it was time to start laying the clothes carefully into the suitcases. But first a more important job. I picked up a small paper bag and gently withdrew a length of bright yellow ribbon that I had purchased some time before. I cut it in half, and carefully tied the first half around the handle of one of the suitcases. I then proceeded to do the same with the other case. I knew that this would be easier to spot at the airports 'carousel', where we would collect our suitcases at the end of our journey. But the real reason I had bought it was, because for me it represented a person's 'coming home'. Wasn't I, in a very real sense, 'coming home'?

Depressed thoughts wafted over me, as I thought once more of my step-father. How on earth would I get around the fact of going 'missing' for two weeks? Eventually I overcame the problem, by sending him a note, saying that I was with friends. As soon as I had written it, I ran across the road, and hurriedly posted it, breathing a sigh of relief, as another hurdle was overcome.

Chris had offered to take us to the airport. Suddenly everything seemed to be slotting into place, things had been gradually sorted out, and I felt a calmness come over me.

I awoke the next morning from a fitful sleep, tossing and turning, with anxious thoughts of what lay ahead. The children dashed about the house excitedly, checking their own bags for anything they might have forgotten. I had taken our English Setter dog, 'Lucy' along to our neighbours, feeling sad at leaving her.

The phone was ringing. It was the American T.V. Company, NBC.

"Norma?" It was Mal Redding, their reporter.

"It's a shame to let such a good story go by. Would your father meet you at the airport?" He said.

"Look, there's no way that I can get in touch with him." I said sadly, thinking about the precious memories a film would have held.

Finally, our luggage was loaded, and we clambered aboard

Chris's car and at last we were on our way. I knew that I would never be fully at ease until we had walked through the departure lounge at the airport.

On the journey, Chris said, "Look, Norma, if you don't like it there and want to leave, what will you do?" She turned to me.

"Yes, I have thought about it, and decided that we would have to go into a Travel Lodge, somewhere." I frowned, hoping that wouldn't happen.

She spoke again,

"I hope you don't mind, but I rang my cousin Kathy, who lives in Los Angeles, and she said to tell you that if you're not happy, you're to make your way down to them," and she quickly passed me a slip of paper, with the address on.

"Oh, that would be wonderful! It would be so nice for me to know that I had a 'bolt hole', a welcoming place, from someone who is your relative," I laughed gratefully.

I looked out of the car window at the bright sunshine, and somehow knew that this incredible journey that I was about to make, was going to change me forever!

On our arrival at the airport, we quickly deposited our suitcases and had some breakfast. After that, we made our way through the crowded terminal and towards the x-ray machines that were situated in front of the departure lounge. I looked at the Airport Personnel. They had no idea what a momentous occasion this was. I wanted to turn and speak to them, and for a second I almost did, but then decided that they looked so busy, I had better not.

Finally it was our turn to pass through the machine, and with a lump in my throat, I turned to say goodbye to my friend. She had supported me so much, how would I ever repay her?

We hugged each other, and I turned away, but turned back as she called out,

"Good luck, Norm. Have a great time!"

With tears in my eyes, I gave an excited wave, and disappeared from view.

The time had come to board the plane. I glanced around at everyone, watching them stowing their hand luggage in the holds above their heads. Can they not understand what's happening? I thought. I'm going to meet my father! I've searched for this man for seven years, at first with only the name of Larry.

Excitement overwhelmed me, and I put out my hand and touched a passing Hostess, "I'm going to meet my father for the very first time!" I blurted out!

She looked at me for a second, "Oh, that's very nice for you."

I realised that she wouldn't understand the enormity of it. No one would, only me!

Many hours later, as I gazed out of the porthole window, I felt my stomach turn over as I realised that we were actually descending through the twilight sky. I looked across at my children. I could see that they were very tired, but how good they had been. I smiled to myself.

After the plane had landed in San Francisco, I thought again of how I should be entering America as an American citizen. But I soon passed those off, as smiling now, I watched my yellow ribbons, and my suitcases come into view! I blinked away the tiredness, as suddenly there was Philip, waiting as he had promised. I felt so relieved. At least Philip would take the strain from me for a little while.

It was dark outside, as we made our way to Philip's brand new Buick. Hayley and Adam collapsed into the softness of the back seat, where two San Francisco caps were waiting for them!

We chatted with excitement, as we headed out to Santa Rosa,

where Philip lived. He smiled as he said, "It will be about an hour's drive, Norma Jean."

"Oh, Philip I didn't realise that you lived that far!" I hated to put people out of their way.

As we drove swiftly along, I stared all around me, feeling strange. Everything was so different. Then, suddenly, I could see bright lights ahead. I was puzzled. What's that? I thought to myself. Then I turned to nudge the children.

"Look, look!" I said excitedly.

"It's the 'Golden Gate' Bridge!" I grinned. I hadn't given it a thought that we might go over it.

"Philip, could we possibly stop please? I would love to get a photo." I turned to him.

As we clambered out of the car, I looked at the amazed faces of the children, and felt warm inside.

It wasn't long before we were settling into bed at Philip's house, all feelings of strangeness just falling away, and we fell immediately into a deep sleep.

The next morning as I opened my eyes, my stomach turned over as I thought about this special day. This was the day I'd be meeting my father. Again doubts about our meeting wafted over me. What if we don't like each other? We were to stay with him for two weeks. That was a long time with someone you didn't know. I bit my lip, maybe I was too optimistic, too ambitious about this? Well, it's too late now, I thought.

After breakfast, we climbed once more into Philip's luxurious car. I ran my fingers over the soft velvet interior, I had never known such comfort.

Philip spoke, "Norma Jean, I'll just go over what I mentioned last night. I spoke to your new brother, Peter, on the phone, and we arranged between us, that once we get to a town called Anderson, I will phone him and he will come to collect you all." He smiled.

My stomach was in knots, as I looked across at Philip.

"Will my father be with him, Philip?" My father! It seemed strange to be saying that now.

"I'm not sure about that. I know that Peter said that he would be taking you to your sister Mary's place."

I began to feel very uneasy. It was beginning to slowly dawn on me that I was going to meet a sister that I had never known about all my life. And she was about to meet me. I tried to forget about the enormity of it all, telling myself that our meeting was still a very long way off, yet.

As the car sped along, I stared out at the alien scenery, trying to absorb everything. I never wanted to forget this day, ever. I wanted to imprint the journey and my feelings as I met my father, forever in my mind.

As we travelled, my thoughts turned to my new siblings. I wondered if they would like me? I had extra worries about my older brother, Harvey, who lived in Kansas. He had been born during the war, and in a sense my mother's affair with our father must have affected him in some way, I thought.

I didn't even know if Harvey actually knew about my existence. Maybe he hadn't been told, as he did live so far away from the rest of the family.

I had spoken to Peter, and he had written to me. I knew from his reactions that he was very happy to have a new English sister!

I had no idea how Mary would feel. I would imagine she would feel very odd about it. One day she only had two brothers, then suddenly she had another sister. I hoped that she didn't feel resentment towards me. She had known our father all her life, and I had never known him at all. I had been thrilled when I heard that I had another sister. I hoped that I would be able to tell her that some time. I was going to spend two weeks with her father, our father, and maybe she wouldn't care for that reality?

I felt a sadness as I thought that it might be the only two weeks that I would ever spend with our father, the only time we would ever meet.

I wondered if Harvey would fly out to meet me, you never know? I smiled to myself.

We decided to take a much needed stop on our way to Anderson. We needed to stretch our legs, and get something to eat. After a short while we were on our way again. I noticed that the landscape was gradually changing. In the beginning we had driven through quite hilly country, then as if in direct contrast, and almost as if a line had been drawn across the land, it evened itself into the flatness of the plain. I noticed that this flatness continued for quite a long way, for many miles. Then very slowly the road we were travelling along began to rise again, only this time, as I looked across to the horizon, it rose into the awe-inspiring, mountainous regions of my father's dwelling place. Later I learnt that those mountains were Shasta and Lassen, non active volcanoes.

My stomach was feeling quite tight by this time. We were almost at Anderson, and I was feeling very anxious as I looked out at the passing traffic. I noticed the pavements shimmering from the heat, and thought how lucky we were to be in the cool of Philip's car. I couldn't comprehend that we were almost at our rendezvous. Suddenly Philip turned off the busy main highway onto a side street, near an open rail-road track. He stopped the car, and I had these strange feelings of not wanting to get out, preferring to stay in the safety of his vehicle.

The heat hit me as we stepped out of the car. I squinted against the bright sunshine, and fumbled in my bag for my sunglasses. I watched as the children ran to peer into a nearby shop window, and I walked round the car to speak with Philip.

"I'll just go and call Peter, I can see a call box over there." My gaze followed where he was pointing.

I stared all around me, all the time my stomach was turning over and over, with nervousness. I could see in the distance the shimmer of a train ambling along its track at the side of the road. The hoot of the locomotive, warning everyone of its presence as it moved slowly through the town. I glanced across at my children huddled together, looking like waifs in a storm.

I looked up, and suddenly thought, what the HELL am I doing here? I must be absolutely mad! I felt as if I had just woken up on another planet. I don't even know where we will be sleeping tonight! Here we were thousands of miles away from home, and Philip was about to leave us. Tears filled my eyes. I just want to go home, I thought.

I wiped my eyes, and noticed Philip walking back towards me, looking extremely pleased. As he reached us, I blurted out, "Philip, I've changed my mind, I want to go home!" I wailed.

For a fleeting moment, his smiled faded, perhaps wondering if I was playing some kind of English joke! Recovering himself, he said, "I've spoken to Peter and he's on his way!"

My heart lurched again. "Look, Philip, I don't think that I want to go through with this. I've changed my mind," I repeated again.

He laughed back at me, "He'll probably drive up in some rusty old pickup truck, and you'll have to throw your bags in the back and clamber in after them!"

I looked up at Philip's tall frame, and nodded, laughing now. I had just visualized myself holding on to the sides of this 'pick-up' truck, and cocking one leg up, in order to try to climb in!

Gone would be the genteel Norma Jean, with her white shorts on! I thought.

I was feeling really afraid now, as we stood together scanning the highway for an unknown car. Suddenly Philip shouted against the noise of the traffic .

"Is this him?"

A bronze coloured car turned quickly in to the side road, and screeched to a halt beside us! I looked at the smiling young man, through his open car window, and knew at once that it was my half-brother, Peter!

I bent towards the window and said, "Hello, Peter, little brother!"

"Hi, Norma Jean!" His eyes twinkled!

"Get yourself out of that car, so that I can give you a big hug!" I was already feeling like the big, bossy, older sister!

I turned around and introduced Philip, at the same time handing him my camera as Peter clambered out of his car!

In a few seconds we were laughingly holding each other, hugging and kissing. I was overcome with emotion as I turned towards the children. Shyly they made their way towards their new uncle, I could sense their apprehension, but knew that it would pass!

Meanwhile, Philip had taken some photos and now it was his turn as he came towards Peter and heartily shook his hand. After a few more words, I felt excitement rising in me, as I thought about my next meeting, and that was going to be with my father!

Philip and I walked together towards the car. I felt a lump in my throat and tears filled my eyes as I knew it was time to say goodbye.

"Well, Norma Jean, I'd better get going," he said.

I felt in a daze, for a second I once again wanted to feel the security of Philip's car, and not the strangeness of Peter's.

Philip spoke again, "Phone me when you can, let me know how you are. I know that you are going to be alright, I can tell."

"I don't know how to thank you Philip, you have been so kind to us." I wiped my eyes with a tissue.

Just before he leaned over to get into his car, he said, "Bye, have a great time!" and turned to wave.

I shouted back, "Next time you're in England, you must have a roast dinner with us!" and laughed.

For a few seconds, I stood and watched him as he drove off up the highway and disappeared out of sight.

I turned around quickly and hurried back to Peter's car, where to my surprise, my luggage had been placed in the car boot, and the children were already settled in the back. I took one last look at the town of Anderson, at the flat-roofed buildings that surround the area. Taking a deep breath, I ducked my head and got into the car, and began to prepare myself to meet my father. We chatted away, as Peter accelerated along the road, my stomach churning all the way. We were nearing Redding, where my sister Mary, lived.

Was I really going to meet this man? Was it really going to happen? This man that my mother once loved. My mountain, that had once seemed insurmountable, had been conquered. I held on tightly as we sped along the road!

CHAPTER 19

As we sat in Peter's car, I could feel an urgency in his driving. I turned to look at the children, and became aware of the worry etched on their faces. For a brief moment, I felt a pang of guilt, wondering if I had been fair to them. I gave them both a reassuring pat, hoping that they would know that it would be alright.

I breathed a sigh, as once again I thought of my contingency plans, my 'bolt-hole' in Los-Angeles, just in case things went wrong. Strange flat-roofed buildings flashed by on our way to Redding. I could see that my sister lived in a poor area. It was so hot, I thought, as sweat trickled slowly down the back of my neck, which I briskly wiped away. All the time Peter and I talked about each other's lives, while my stomach kept churning!

While Peter was driving, I kept glancing across at him, trying to see a resemblance between us. I could see that we had similar noses. I wondered if it was the same nose as our father's.

"We're almost there now, our father is waiting at Mary's for you," Peter said, reinforcing what I already knew. My stomach lurched again! My father is waiting for me! How did I get myself into this? What on earth was I thinking of? Your gut-feelings brought you here, thats what! I said to myself.

Peter was gradually slowing the car down, and I was feeling extremely nervous, fiddling with my bag.

I glanced once more out of the car window as we drew up outside Mary's bungalow home. I quickly opened the door and stepped out into the brilliant sunshine. Once again the heat hit me. It must be a hundred degrees, I thought. I noticed that there were three sides surrounding the yard, enclosed by a wire fence and a mesh gate. I followed Peter up the path, which was strewn with children's toys. By then I could feel the heat burning my nostrils.

A large black dog ambled up to me, and seeming to approve, wagged its tail. By this time my legs were propelling me along, as I stepped onto an old wooden porch and through a squeaky swing door. The room that I was entering was very dark, compared with the brightness of the sunshine outside. I noticed an old fashioned fan slowly turning, unconcerned with the importance of the day!

I saw nothing then! My children, the family, nothing. Everything fell away from me, and with a kind of tunnel vision, I set my sights on a grey-haired man rising slowly from a chair at the far end of the room. I took a deep breath and moved slowly towards him. He too came forward, shaking his head and smiling. With tears in my eyes, I noticed how tall he seemed, against my five foot three inches. We stood for a split second facing each other, and I lifted my head and looked up into his eyes, eyes that mirrored my own.

"With a broad smile, I said, "You're a hard man to track down, Dad!" remembering that it was okay to call him that.

He grinned, saying, "Hi, my darlin' daughter!"

Then we were in each other's arms, laughing and crying, as all the tension of the last few weeks disappeared. Then I remembered the children, patiently standing behind me. Suddenly there was a buzz, as if everyone had just come to life! I had imagined this happening so many times, and now it really was!

I turned and introduced the children to their American Grandfather, at last!

My father led me by the arm to my waiting sister, Mary. She was sitting by the table, and I felt overcome with shyness, as I bent over to kiss her, and noticed immediately her high cheek bones, similar to mine.

"Hello, Mary, little sister!" I said laughing!

"Well, hello, Norma Jean, how are you?" I noticed how nice her voice sounded.

Tears filled my eyes again, when I thought of all the years that had gone by, and we never knew about each other. I realised that Mary probably didn't see the sentiment quite like I did, after all, she was a lot younger than me and had been surrounded by her family.

I sank down into the armchair as Mary and I continued to chat about my journey, and how I managed to get there. Gradually Mary's children moved towards me, trying to get a look at their new English auntie.

I smiled as I noticed Hayley and Adam, rummaging now in the bag that contained the presents we'd bought in Oxford Street, London, for the family. I watched my father, sitting in the chair opposite me.

Occasionally he would look across, and shake his head. I tried to notice if we were alike. It had been a burning desire in me, all the years of my search, and now I would be able, in the next few days, to truly find out our likenesses.

I thought about Harvey, my brother in Kansas.

I looked at my father and said, "Does Harvey know anything about me, Dad?" I smiled.

He smiled across at me, saying, "Harvey just phoned here

about five minutes before you came, Norma Jean. He was real sorry that he missed you." I felt a warmth come over me, so he does know.

My father continued,

"He couldn't believe that you were already here, in California. He's going to ring at 3pm on Sunday."

I sighed, thank goodness he knows, and he wants to speak to me. I began to look forward to Sunday and to making contact with my last sibling.

I noticed the cats, seeming to be everywhere. I adore all animals, and they were obviously in a loving home. I watched as one of them trod very gently across my armchair, and purring contentedly, curled up in a soft ball on my lap, and promptly went to sleep!

As I looked around at everyone, I was feeling very strange. An intense weariness flooded through me, and I knew that we still had at least an hour's journey up my father's mountain, to Weaverville, where my father lived.

I caught my father's eye,

"Dad, would you mind if we went soon?" It was so strange to be calling this man Dad, but I was very happy to do that!

I continued, "We're really tired, and it would be nice to see the mountains in daylight." I smiled, looking again at his eyes. They are like mine, I realised.

"Sure, honey, whenever you're ready." And he slowly stood up. After a few minutes more, we all made our way back out into the brilliant sunshine. I suddenly remembered my camera, and hurriedly rummaged in my bag.

I could see that I would have to take charge, and began organising everyone into some sort of camera call. As I stood beside Mary, I looked up at her, she was so much taller than I.

"Honey, Mary takes after her mother's side of the family,

and Indians are not very tall anyway!" our father said, and we all laughed!

After that, I turned around to witness my father hauling our suitcases from Peter's car, and placing them into a gleaming, white, estate car. Obviously his pride and joy! We were finally ready to be off, and with plans to meet on Sunday, we waved goodbye.

Again a real strangeness came over me, I turned to the children sitting shyly in the back, and reassured them with a smile. I kept giving my father sideways glances as we drove along. I could see some similarities, especially from the side. We seemed to have the same profile.

Dad and I talked as we drove along. I looked all around me, watching the scenery change once more, as we began the ascent up the twisting narrow roads that led up the mountain. I took a sharp intake of breath, as I absorbed the spectacular scenery! We drove very close to the edge and I felt my stomach go over as I glanced down into the valley. I looked across at my father and then glanced back at the children. I suddenly thought, I don't even know what sort of driver this man is, as I put my foot down hard on an imaginery brake! I've used up a lot of my life, but my children haven't! I put those thoughts out of my mind, as I pulled down the sun-visor. The reds and golds of the setting sun, were amazing, as if the heavens themselves were on fire. I glanced again at this man, my elusive father. Perhaps he doesn't want us to stay for two weeks, I hadn't given him much option, had I? Maybe we should just stay for a couple of days, as thoughts of my bolthole came into my mind.

"What wonderful scenery, Dad." I turned to look at him. There were 'Christmas' trees everywhere. I ducked my head down, and lifted my eyes and it seemed to me that those trees were touching the sky!

"You know, Norma Jean, for five dollars, you can go and cut down your own Christmas tree, any size you like."

As I listened to him, I began to notice that there were hardly any barriers to stop people in their cars from going over the side. Don't look, I said to myself, as I glanced away.

At last we entered the main street of Weaverville. I could see what a beautiful town it was, and full of history. As we drove up the wide street, I turned my head from side to side, not wanting to miss anything. Suddenly, my mouth dropped open,

"Oh, Hayley and Adam, look at that quaint cinema. It must have been there from the time the town was built." I smiled back at them.

"Weaverville is very different from Redding, Dad."

"I love it here, honey. I've been here since just after the war. I worked in the lumber mill here."

I already knew that we were going to have a great time exploring the next day!

Finally, my father swung his gleaming car into the yard beside his house. As I opened the car door, an old buff-coloured dog strolled up to greet us.

"Thats 'Pippie', one of my dogs," my father said, as he hauled one of the suitcases out of the back of the car. I felt a pang of guilt as I watched him. I'd packed so many clothes, I had no idea what the weather would be like here in the mountains. I could see that my father's house was situated directly on the road. It reminded me of a Spanish hacienda. My father had rented the large detached house for many years. We entered the front door, which faced the road, and another dog, a black and brown creature, came to greet us.

"That's 'Mottie' and the cat's name is 'Foot'. I gave my pets Indian names," my father laughed.

It was nice to have the animals there, it would ease our strangeness. I stared around me, noticing my father's pictures on the wall of his other children. Maybe my picture will be beside my siblings, one day, I said silently to myself.

Meanwhile, my father bustled about, excitedly showing us into each room, and where we would be sleeping that night. It was good of him to invite us there; after all he didn't know us, did he?

We followed Dad upstairs.

"This will be where you'll sleep, Adam." He smiled at him. We peered into the room, looking at the large double bed that was going to be Adam's for the visit. Dad then turned and showed us the bathroom and another large bedroom, before we followed him back downstairs to another bedroom that was just off the lounge. In it was a large, king-sized bed. "Honey, that's where you and Hayley will sleep."

I was feeling so drained. Later, after I'd settled the children into bed, I sank into the armchair exhausted. Dad sat wearily in the armchair opposite mine and I sensed that we would now begin to really get to know each other.

I looked slowly around his comfortable front room, and imagined my brothers and sister growing up there. My father began to speak about his life, and about his wife and family. He then began to talk of my mother, as I knew he eventually would.

He said, "You know, Norma Jean, I never was stationed with Carl, at Stansted Airport, I was stationed in France." My mouth dropped open. I felt stunned. All those years that I had searched there, hoping and praying that I would find his name on a list somewhere.

"I was stationed at Calais, France. That's where I met your uncle, Carl Wraley, who was married to your aunt June. We were given a furlough, a holiday, and so Carl asked me to come to England to meet his English wife's family. I was really pleased to go to England, and that's where I met your mother."

All this time I'd been transfixed, straining my ears, to make sure that I didn't miss anything. To understand the story at last.

"Your mother opened the door to me, and I couldn't get over how beautiful she was! I tried to light a cigarette, and fumbled in my pockets looking for a match, but my hands were shaking so much!" We both laughed.

"After that we liked each other's company so much, that, for the time that I was there, we went everywhere together. We got along real swell!" He looked across wistfully at me.

"You know, Norma Jean, I was actually born in Warsaw, Missouri."

I was shocked! I stared at him. "Warsaw?" I said. "I don't believe it! My last resort at trying to find you, was going to be actually putting an advert in the Warsaw newspaper."

I remembered Harold suggesting it. He shook his head in disbelief, then said, "You know, your aunt June was right in a way, about it being Kansas. I went back to visit my mother after the war, she had re-married. Her new surname was Lutman." So that's where the name came from on the payslip. She had re-married. That explained it, I thought.

"Then after that I followed the lumber company out to Weaverville, and we've been here ever since. This is where Mary and Peter were born and raised, and I haven't been anywhere since then." I watched as he raised his cup of black coffee to his lips, and sipped at it.

"Dad, did my middle name come from your mother?"

"Well, her name was Lois; I guess your mom must've known her middle name, and called you after her." I felt warm at that thought.

"Another thing I wanted to ask you, Dad?"

"Fire away, honey." He smiled.

"Are you artistic in any way? I've always enjoyed art. I would come first in it at school."

"Sure, I was real good at art," he replied. I took a deep breath. "In fact, when I was eighteen, I entered an art competition and won several dollars in prize money. A few weeks later, there was a knock at the door, and it was men representing Walt Disney!" I gasped!

"They asked if I would consider going to work for him in Los-Angeles."

"WOW, and what happened?"

"Well, you know, Norma Jean, I was a young man who was having a great time in the mountains, just a-huntin' and a-fishin'. I was having me a ball!" he laughed.

"So what did you decide, Dad?"

"Well, I thought about it a little bit, but in the end I turned the offer down!"

"You turned down Walt Disney?" I stared in disbelief!

He nodded his head, as he said, "Not long after that, along came the war, and I was called up anyhow. That sure put an end to a lot of people's dreams!" he said sadly.

I felt myself relax, and curled my feet up under me, really enjoying my father's company. We talked and talked, until it was quite late. I could feel my eyelids getting heavy, and eventually got up to say goodnight. We hugged each other, as I said, "Goodnight,Dad."

"Goodnight, honey, I'll see you in the morning."

I felt so funny, here I was saying goodnight to this man, calling him Dad, a dad that I had not known about for forty years. I felt awkward, I didn't want him to feel that he had to have us there, because of something that happened so many years ago.

I crawled into bed, beside my sleeping daughter, pulling the covers up all around me, with a hundred thoughts going round in my mind. What were we going to do if we stayed the two whole weeks? This had cost such a lot of money, surely we should try to stay longer than two days? And with that thought, I drifted off to sleep!

CHAPTER 20

Bright sunshine streamed through the window, as I opened my eyes the next morning. In an instant, I remembered exactly where I was. I turned my head to look at my still sleeping daughter, at the same time stretching out my legs and feeling really rested now.

I could hear talking from upstairs and smiled to myself, when I realised that it was Adam talking to his new grandad.

I swung my legs out of the bed, and quickly got dressed. I still felt so strange, questions were still going round in my mind. How would Dad and I get along? I hoped that the children would behave themselves! I turned my head as I thought I could hear a deep voice singing. I strained my ears, and then smiled to myself, as I realised that it was Dad.

"I've got a beautiful daughter, I've got a beautiful daughter!" I could hear him singing. How lovely, I thought. Was my father really singing that about me? Well, maybe we'll stay just a little longer, maybe we'll stay for five days.

I opened the bedroom door, and walked slowly into the front room, suddenly my father rushed towards me, and threw his arms around me saying,

"My English daughter really did sleep here last night," he joked.

It felt so strange to me, that this man, my biological father would want to hold me, just because I was me.

I looked across at my son, who was seated at the table, scooping spoonfuls of cereal into his mouth. Well he seems fine, I thought. In fact he looked extremely happy.

I peered out of the window at the brilliant blue sky.

"Dad, would it be alright if I just take the children for a walk through the town? Maybe we'll buy an ice-cream?" The children let out a whoop of joy!

"Sure, honey, I'll tidy up a bit while you're gone."

I glanced back at my father, I kept having to look at him, and I knew he felt the same. I could see my resemblance to him, especially as my mother had said, around the eyes. I felt thrilled about that.

So the children and I made our way up the main street of Weaverville. The weather was really warm, and I breathed deeply, thinking about the beauty of the town and the surrounding mountains. I really fancied an ice-cream, even though it was early in the morning! The children steered me straight to the ice-cream parlour, where we were to become the most regular customers. We browsed around the shops, and I became totally besotted with the 'American Indian' shops, as I now felt so much a part of them.

My father had told me how Weaverville was an old gold mining town, founded by the Chinese. In fact there was still a Chinese temple, steeped in history, at the far end of the town. As I stood looking at the town, I could sense the past. I imagined what it must have been like, visualizing stage coaches trundling through, hundreds of years before.

We strolled past the old antiquated cinema that we had seen the night before. I cupped my hands and peered through one of the glass windows, we laughed at the simple way that they had advertised their films for the week. Posters with hurriedly written 'titles' in 'felt tip' pens.

Once back at my father's house, we decided that the first thing that we must do, was to drive out to the supermarket situated at the edge of town.

We all jumped into dad's car, as the novelty of being in a foreign land, was just beginning to sink in!

As we entered the supermarket, my father hurriedly grabbed a trolley and began to explain how the store worked. It wasn't long before I realised that there was a 'language barrier'.

"Dad?" I called to him, as he pushed the trolley in front of me.

He turned round.

"Dad, do you possibly know where the choc-ices are?"

He stared at me, his mouth open.

"What, honey?" A puzzled look on his face.

"Choc-ices, Dad, choc-ices?" I raised my voice.

"Choc-aices?" He said, in a funny sort of Cockney/American accent!

As I looked at the expression on his face, I suddenly saw the funny side of it. I felt a rumble of a laugh starting in the pit of my stomach, and the more that I looked at my father's puzzled look, the more I began to laugh, until in the end tears filled my eyes, I was laughing so much!

I began to stride along the supermarket aisles, with my father pushing the trolley and galloping behind me, when eventually we found them, and discovered that they were called 'Eskimo Pies'! We also found that ice lollies were called 'Popsicles', and biscuits were cookies and so on.

Although I knew that we were on our best behaviour, I felt that my father and I were alike in temperament. He seemed to be incredibly patient, as he followed me around the store that day.

Dad decided that we should visit the Trinity River after we

had been to the supermarket.

As soon as this was mentioned to Hayley and Adam, they ran around excitedly, picking up towels and swimsuits, and hurriedly cramming them into a bag.

Once more I found myself clinging onto the side of the car, as Dad wound his way round the mountain. We had prepared a picnic, and as we alighted from the car, I breathed in the pure air, and gazed around at the lush green pine trees sloping gently towards the river.

We had to make quite a steep climb down towards the banks of the river, and the children hurried on ahead. It wasn't long before we heard shrieks of laughter as they plunged into the clear cool water.

My father and I sat and watched them, and as we sat together, he began to talk again of my mother, and then of his Mohawk grandmother. This absolutely fascinated me, it was hard to believe that she was an ancestor of mine too.

"You know, honey?" he said turning to me. "She loved to dance. When I met her, she wanted me to dance with her, but I was far too shy then: but now I regret it!" I felt a pang for him, and wondered what her name was.

He went on, "It's funny, Norma Jean, but I really love dancing and you tell me you do, too!" He smiled.

Two days had passed by, I felt myself gradually unwinding from the tenseness of the days before.

We found Dad, and Grandad, so affectionate, and it was difficult for me, as I had never been used to it.

He would often say, "Let your dad give you some 'sugar' honey?"(His term for affection!)

"I've got a lot of lost years to make up for!" He would laugh.

One day, I said to myself, maybe we'll stay longer than five days, after all I may never get the chance to visit my father again.

I could hear the children's laughter, as he fussed over them, and felt a pang, as they would miss this fuss, once back in England.

It was Sunday, and I looked forward to visiting with Mary and Peter once again. I had felt great excitement at the thought of finally speaking with Harvey, and hoped that we wouldn't run out of things to say to each other.

I cringed at the thought of the drive down the mountain, but I was getting more used to the roads and began to realise that my father actually was an extremely good driver, and with those thoughts, I made a conscious decision to enjoy the drive!

Once again we pulled up in the car, outside Mary's. Dad explained how much hotter Redding is compared to Weaverville, because of the mountains. I stepped out into the seering heat, thinking about the last time I walked up her path, and how different I felt now, compared to then!

Everyone seemed to be bustling about as we walked through the door. My nieces and nephews crowded around us, and I thought how nice it must be for Mary's children, to have relatives from England. Maybe it will make them more interested in English history, and the British people?

"Hayley and Adam?" We turned around. It was Crystal, my oldest, new niece.

"Would you like to help me with my paper round?" she smiled.

Crystal explained that they had to roll the newspaper, and secure it with an elastic band. Then all they had to do was to 'lob' it onto people's front lawns!

"Just like we see in the American films!" laughed Hayley.

With the children gone, I sat right beside the telephone waiting for Harvey. Suddenly the phone rang. "Hello?" I said rather tentatively.

"Is that Norma Jean?" A smooth voice answered.

"Yes," I laughed.

"I'm sorry I just missed you last Friday, Norma Jean, this has all been such a surprise."

"Yes," I replied. "I had a terrible time trying to raise the money to get here. I had to do it right away or I would never have known peace inside my mind. I would have always been wondering about our father."

I relaxed back into the armchair, feeling better now that I was actually talking to him. I still couldn't quite grasp that we were related, that he was an older brother. We discovered, as we talked, that we had similar interests. Harvey liked to dance, he has also a keen interest in writing. He also talked about his life in Kansas University, doing his PHD. I explained how I found philosophy fascinating as well.

I glanced at my wrist watch, suddenly realising that we had been talking for a whole hour!

"Look Harvey, we had better say goodbye. Perhaps you'll come to England one day?"

"You know, Norma Jean, I was in England, in the American Airforce over there. I was stationed near Northampton," he said.

I was stunned! "Harvey, I lived in Northampton for many years!"

"Well, my son Mathew was born at the Barrett Maternity Home there, in 1968!" He sounded shocked.

"That's funny, I used to work in Barclaycard, which was near there. I was only five minutes away at that time!" My mouth dropped open, I just could not believe the coincidence!

"That means that we could have walked straight by each

other!" He laughed.

What a small world, I thought, as I said, "Harvey, I'll write to you when I get back."

"Goodbye little sister."

"Goodbye big brother!" I answered.

Later, Harvey was to tell me, that he actually did book a flight to California, but then had second thoughts, when he thought that it would be better if we had two weeks on our own, getting to know each other. As he said it, I realised that was a very generous thing to do. So all that time that I worried about my older brother bearing me a grudge, I needn't have worried at all.

Later on, I managed to have a talk with Mary. When I first arrived, I had given her a present, now Mary was holding a small box out to me, "Here, Norma Jean, this is for you."

I took the box from her outstretched hand, and gently opened it.

"Oh, Mary, what a lovely, silver ring! Thank you very much, I will always treasure it!" I said, as I kissed her.

A few more days passed by and I found myself drawing nearer to my father. I watched my children and listened as they talked with him.

"Hayley and Adam, the next time you come to Weaverville, your ol' Grandaddy is going to take you huntin' and fishin' in the mountains."

"Great!" They both said.

One evening my father produced a sleek looking shotgun. He began to tell me how he usually goes hunting in September, and about how, when he was younger, he shot a brown bear! I knew that mountain people went hunting and fishing, it was as much a part of their lives as the air is that we breathe.

I had decided now, that we would stay the whole two weeks,

in fact the whole of my feelings had turned around, and I knew that I was not looking forward to going home!

One day, as my father and I walked together down the main street, we bumped into an aquaintance of dad's.

"Hi.... I'd like you to say hello to someone," my father said. "Can you guess who she is?" he smiled.

I blushed slightly as this stranger turned to look at me? "Why, Mac," as they called my father, "it's your daughter, anyone could see that!" he said, laughing.

I could feel myself grinning from ear to ear. I turned to look at my father, and noticed his eyes crinkling with laughter. I knew that I really did look like him, if a perfect stranger could say that! It was amazing, I thought. Throughout the rest of our stay in Weaverville, from time to time, Dad would ask the same question and people would always answer the same, "Why, it's your daughter!!"

For me personally, it set the seal on the relationship with my father.

I had suggested to the children that we should stay the whole two weeks. I watched as their faces lit up and knew that I had made the right decision.

Dad had driven us every day down to the Trinity Lakes. Again the scenery was spectacular, the fresh green pine trees reflected in the lakes like a mirrored image. No wonder they called it 'Gods country' I thought to myself. It was so hot! The sun would pound down on us, and there would be no shelter from the heat of the day! Dad and I would sit together, watching the children swimming and diving. I knew that they would never want to leave.

One day we passed the newspaper offices of the Trinity County Journal.

"You know, Norma Jean, I know one of the reporters there,

her name is Pat Hicks. She and her husband run the drug-store over there." I looked to where he pointed.

"Honey, next time you're in the drug-store, buying something, why don't you mention us to her? It sure would make a good story for the newspaper."

I turned my head and looked at my father. He's really accepting me now, I thought. I would have liked to go to the local newspaper, but never would have done so unless he had suggested it.

So the very next day, I entered the old fashioned drug-store. As I stepped over the threshold, history wafted over me, just as if I'd been through a timewarp. The odours of all the different objects were carried on the air, permeating everything in the store. As I made my way across the timbered floor, I noticed different jars displayed on shelves, and I imagined it must have been just like this a hundred years before. I caught the eye of Mr Hicks, the pharmacist, and began to relate to him my story. I noticed that he was looking at me in a strange way, and I could understand why. After all, here I was a woman saying that I was all the way from London, England, and claiming to be 'Mac' McCloud's daughter! As I was speaking to him, it sounded pretty unreal to me, let alone him.

"Well, Mrs Clarke, Pat Hicks isn't here at the moment. Wow, what you are saying! Are you sure that it will be alright with 'Mac'?"

"Yes," I laughed! "My father said that it would be okay!"

"Well, I'll sure remember to tell Pat when she comes in. I'm sure she'll be in touch!"

Later that same day, there was a knock on my father's front door. I peered round it, and there was my father and Mr Hicks, talking in quiet tones. I laughed to myself, as I guessed that Mr Hicks was just checking my story!

Mr Hicks stepped into the house.

"Pat says, if it's okay, can you go to the drug-store this afternoon?" He shuffled his feet.

"Sure, if that's okay with Norma Jean?" He turned towards me, and I nodded my head.

At 2pm, Dad and I entered the drug-store. I noticed a lady walking towards us, and realised that it must be Pat. Her genial character put me at my ease immediately as we shook hands. After a few moments, Pat went behind the old counter, and picking up her note-pad and pen said, "Right, Norma Jean, where shall we begin?"

For the next hour, with Dad standing beside me, I began to steadily relate the story of my search. At the point where I got to the trauma of my wedding day, I watched, frowning, as Pat softly laid down her pad and pen, and moved back round the counter towards me. Suddenly and with arms outstretched, she said, "Oh, Norma Jean, you deserve a BIG HUG!" Tears filled my eyes as I warmed to her compassion, and we stood for a short time hugging each other. My father watched in amazement at us both, and having only just met!

A week later our story, plus a picture, was shown in the TRINITY COUNTY JOURNAL.

Time seemed to be going so quickly now, I didn't like to think about leaving, and would push those thoughts firmly from my mind.

One day, Dad talked about all of us going to the Trinity County Fair, which was held every year on the other side of the mountain. We were very excited about this, and really looked forward to it. Dad's lady friend, Sue Bailey, whom we'd met before, was coming with us.

We all set off with great excitement, thinking about the kind of experiences we would have that day.

The heat was stifling as we alighted from the car. I fumbled in my bag for my sunglasses. On our arrival at the gates, the fair seemed simular to the ones that we have in England, but as we ambled through I could see that it was quite different.

Dad and I sauntered along, sometimes arm in arm, as he excitedly pointed out all the different things that were on show. People milled around and I watched everyone as they bustled about in the hot sunshine.

For a time we watched the live-stock show, until Hayley and Adam pestered me so much, that I had to take them to the fairground proper. Hayley tried the basket-ball and jumped up and down as she won two stuffed cows! I slumped down on a bale of hay, as a feeling of total unreality wafted over me once more. Was this a dream? Would I be waking up in my bed, in England!

As I browsed around the American Indian stalls, wishing that I had more money to spend, a huge 'brown bear' moved at an easy pace in front of me. I knew that the 'bear' was Trinity County's emblem for forest fires. Many years ago there had been a major forest fire, and when the last flame had been doused, all that was left of the wild life was a small brown bear. They named him 'Smokey' and adopted him as their emblem, their fight against forest fires.

Suddenly we turned around as we heard 'whoops' of joy from behind us. I opened my eyes wide, as I saw a row of people cramming pies into their mouths in the 'pie eating' contest! I was amazed, as I had never witnessed anything quite like it!

I glanced down at my watch and lifted my eyes to the horizon. I noticed that the heat was finally leaving the setting sun, and felt a pang, as I knew it was time to leave. We all felt extremely fatigued as we strolled towards the gates and out to the car.

I turned to take one last lingering look at the Trinity Fair, what a wonderful day we have had, I sighed. Would I ever return? I wondered sadly. Optimism took over, and my spirits rose, as I thought, of course we will! And we began our journey back around the mountain to my father's home.

CHAPTER 21

"Honey, I want you to think very seriously about coming to live in America." My father looked across at me, as we sat together. We were almost at the end of our holiday, and my father, like me, was trying to come to terms with saying goodbye.

"This can't be the end, honey, the only time we'll ever meet?" He said sadly.

I watched 'Foot' the cat, as she rolled over and over on my navy sandal shoe, laughing as she tried to stick her soft furry nose up into the toe. How we would miss everything! We would miss the dogs, 'Pippie' and 'Mottie'. And how we would miss the spectacular scenery.

I thought with a poignancy about my life, and if I'd grown up as an American. How different my life would have been. But I knew that I was very British and my roots were in England, but I was sorely tempted then, to just pack up and move to Weaverville, for I loved it there!

I was half-American, and I knew that when I got back I was going to have a fight on my hands, to claim what was rightfully mine, my American citizenship!

It was the day before our departure to San Francisco. I watched my father sitting at the table, "I'm going to write a letter to Pamela Winfield, honey." I smiled at him.

Later on, he turned to me, "Here, honey, what do you think?" His eyes crinkled.

I read:

Dear Mrs Pamela Winfield,

I am very pleased to write to thank you for your dedicated help to my very beautiful and precious daughter, Norma Jean Clarke, whom I love so very much, in her search those seven long years for her father, ME. I had no idea whatsoever that I had a daughter in England. I am sure glad that Norma Jean didn't give up her search for me, because it would also have been my loss. God Bless you all. Her brothers and sister over here love her too. And Norma's children, Hayley and Adam, my grandchildren, are truly loved by me and my American family.

I hope other G.I.'S find their children as I did, it's a feeling beyond belief!

Thank you Pamela and all who helped her.
I love you all. And God bless you and help you.
Lawrence H. McCloud.
A happy, happy, man!

A lump rose up in my throat as I read his letter. What a wonderful letter, I thought. Straight from his heart. It was as if we had always known each other, and yet we hadn't. I tucked the letter carefully away in my bag, and replied, "It's such a lovely letter, she'll be really pleased." Tears filled my eyes.

Later, my father suggested that he wanted to take me to his church, high up on the hill. We came out of the house into the warm air.

The father and the daughter were standing together, side by side, at the top of the mountain! But for the daughter's tenacity, they may never have met!

After a time, we arrived at the old wooden church, which stood majestically overlooking the old town. As I shook hands with father Lawrence, he began to explain the history and the type of services that were held there.

"It's wonderful, Dad," I said, as I stood looking at the white painted, wooden church. Just like we see in the films, I thought.

Now it was time to return to my father's house, and begin to pack our clothes. I just couldn't shake of the feeling of despondency. We had been to say goodbye to Mary, Peter and their families. I had no idea if we would ever meet any of them again, or if I'd get to meet my father again, either.

I worried about my father. He had lived alone since his wife had died, and since our arrival, this house had been so noisy, so full of life! How lonely would he be? I wondered.

My journey to reach this place had taken me almost seven gruelling years. I thought about all the wonderful people that I had met along the way. From the bottom of my heart, I thanked them. It had taken me a lot of soul-searching on my journey, but there had come within me a huge transformation. I now know, that I had been suppressed. I now know, that I had been mentally, verbally, and emotionally abused. But I am spirited, I am strong. I made up my mind that I would not let my search beat me! I had been re-born, I had just begun to live!

I bent down and ran my fingers underneath my father's big bed, checking for anything left there. I noticed how subdued the children were, as they helped to take the bags out to the car. I glanced around the room for one last time, then bending down, I kissed 'Foot' and 'Mottie' on the top of their heads. I turned and hurried out of the door.

The children sat in the back of dad's car, having already said their goodbye's to the pets. For a minute I stood and looked at my father's house, I would never forget it, but would I ever visit it again?

"Honey, you must know how hard this is to take you to the

bus-station. I don't want you to go." I heard his voice break.

Side by side, in thoughtful silence, we journeyed through the town of Weaverville one more time.

"I don't want to leave, Dad, it's so wonderful here, but we have to go back home," I answered softly.

I looked up at the mountains, and then noticed that we were driving past the supermarket, where we had laughed so much at the 'language barrier' and my father's pronounciation of "choc-aices" instead of choc-ices! Had I really only wanted to stay for just two days? It seemed ridiculous now!

Once again, I took a long, last, lingering look at the mountains that surrounded the town. I sighed, there was no snow on them. How I wished that I could see them covered in a white blanket, against a blue sky.

As my father drove slowly back down the mountain, I tried to take in every last detail of 'Gods country' and imprint it forever on my memory, so that I would never, ever forget it!

We were making our way back to Redding, and the Greyhound Bus-station. From there we would travel on the bus for around seven hours, to San Francisco. Then it was into the Travel Lodge, adjacent to the Airport. I hoped that the swimming pool there, would be a sort of distraction from our leaving California.

Mary had said that she would not be at the Bus-station, but Peter said he would try to make it.

He was the first of my new family, to make contact with me. I smiled to myself, as I thought of his midnight telephone call, many months ago.

At last my father swung his gleaming white car into the Bus-station. My stomach was in knots. I tried to put our leaving each other to the back of my mind, and began to organise the children. With my father's help, we hauled the luggage through the double glass doors of the Bus-station, and entered the bustling departure lounge.

I glanced all around for Peter, but feeling despondent at not seeing him, turned to look at the tickets that I held in my hand.

Suddenly my father's voice came to me,

"Norma-Jean, I'm going to get a coffee. Are you okay, honey?"

I saw the sorrowful look on his face, and a lump came up in my throat.

"Okay, Dad, when I've got this sorted out I'll come to look for you." I forced a smile.

Meanwhile, the children had dashed off to find a restroom, and worried now, I stood on tiptoe, hoping to catch a glimpse of them.

"I bet they are playing on the computer games!" I mumbled to myself.

Suddenly, a voice sounded over the Tannoy system, telling travellers to board the bus for San Francisco!

I felt myself beginning to panic, as there was no sign of the children, and none of my father or Peter, either.

I had handed in the cases now, and felt an urgency as I began to run through the crowded departure area, my eyes scanning the cafe. Suddenly Hayley and Adam appeared into view! I breathed a sigh of relief, as at the same time I caught sight of my father, sitting, his shoulders hunched, sipping his coffee. He sat with his back to me, and for a brief second I hesitated to speak to him, for the time had come to finally say goodbye.

I stretched out my hand, tentatively, and lightly touched his shoulder.

"Dad, we've got to go, they've called our bus!" I said urgently.

He stood up immediately and a lump came up in my throat,

as I noticed that he had been crying. He followed us quickly through the crowds, all the time I looked around for Peter. By this time I felt so choked up that I was finding it hard to swallow.

We reached the barrier, where only travellers were allowed through, tears stung my eyes, and began to trickle down my face. I could contain them no longer. My father too, was openly crying. I turned towards him, and we hugged each other.

"Well," I said between sobs, "Well, this is it, Dad. Will you try to come to England sometime?" I wiped at my eyes.

He withdrew his own hankie from his pocket, and nodded his head, as he too wiped his eyes.

Now it was the children's turn, and they threw their arms around him, as he bent to kiss them goodbye.

"Norma Jean?" He raised his voice.

"Look, honey, I can't wait to see the bus go, you don't mind, do you? I can't stand to watch you leave."

"Of course not, Dad, it would be better, really."

I tried to smile.

I turned round quickly, my legs propelling me, as I headed for the Greyhound Bus. I suddenly realised that I could hear my father's voice, shouting. I turned back, "Norma Jean, we will write! We will make the ocean HOT with our letters!" And with his words still in the air, he turned away, and headed back to the departure area.

Again, I began to cry. I didn't seem to be able to stop it as I hustled the children on board the Bus. I followed the children up the steps and walked along the gangway. I ducked my head to look out of the window, and my heart lurched as I saw my father in the distance, with his face buried in his hanky, openly weeping. I watched for a last glimpse of him, before he disappeared through the doors of the terminal, and out of sight.

We were now seated, and I was trying really hard to calm myself down, by concentrating on our long journey ahead. Suddenly someone appeared in front of us, and I quickly realised that it was a friend of Peter's.

I gasped!

"Where's Peter?" I said, as I stood up and peered out of the windows once more. In a second I spotted him, sprinting across the tarmac, dodging in and out of people! I turned and pushed my way back down the aisle of the bus, jumping the three steps down to the ground! We rushed towards each other, until we caught and held each other tight!

I looked at Peter, both of us shedding tears. I realised that he was not ashamed to cry openly.

"Norma Jean, you must come back as soon as possible. You belong here with us, we are your family."

He was really serious. "I'll think about it, Peter, but it's a big step!" I smiled through my tears.

Here we were, I thought, brother and sister, from different countries, with different cultures, and even some of the time, a different language! There was the vastness of an ocean, and a huge expanse of land between us. Could this ever be bridged? I asked myself? Well, there was a good possibility.

"Oh, Norma Jean, I wished you'd been around as we were growing up." He wiped his eyes.

I truly felt then like the big, older sister.

"Peter, I will write to you!" I tried to smile, feeling a deep sadness.

I turned my head as I could hear the Bus driver calling me. I didn't think that I had any more tears left in me as I turned to hug Peter one more time.

"Goodbye, Peter."

"Goodbye, Norma Jean."

I turned away from him, and clambered back on board the bus, towards my anxious children.

I pressed my face against the window as the Bus left the station. I strained to get one last look at Peter, waving from a distance. I quickly lifted my hand and with the briefest of waves, he had disappeared and the Bus was on its way to San Francisco.

As I sat there, I thought about my father, and that he would by now, be on his way back up his mountain. I thought about the nature of things, and how this trip had changed us all. It had not only changed me, but my father, Peter, Mary, and their families, and I believed that it would have even changed Harvey, who I had only spoken to on the phone. Yes, I thought, it has changed us all.

The next day, I sat stunned, staring wide eyed out of the aircraft window. I lent over and, craning my neck, I lifted my eyes as I tried to get one last look at the bay and the hills that surround San Francisco. I strained my eyes, trying to see my father's mountain, an impossibility, but I tried just the same!

"Mum." I turned to look at my young son speaking to me. "Mum, we won't really miss grandad, will we?"

"Why do you say that, Adam?" I smiled at him.

"Cos, your just like him, that's why!" Tears filled my eyes at his poignant words.

I thought about my father sitting alone in his armchair, with his cat 'Foot' curled up on his lap, and his dog 'Mottie' laid at his feet. I knew that he would be feeling terribly lonely.

Again I could hear his voice calling to me, "Norma Jean, we will make the ocean HOT with our letters!"

Well, I thought, I was going to make sure that we did!

People might say that you shouldn't disturb your past, and yes, I took a very great risk, I thought, as I wiped a tear from my eye, but at least I have no regrets. I now felt whole, I felt complete.

After all, I told myself so many years ago, there *could* be a 'happy ending', how would I ever know unless I tried?

ENDS

ADDRESSES

TRACE: Sophia Byrne, membership secretary.
11 St. Tewdrick's Place,
Mathern,
Nr. Chepstow,
Gwent, NT6 6JW
U.K.

NATIONAL PERSONNEL RECORDS CENTRE:
9700 Page Blvd.,
St. Louis,
MO 63132
U.S.A.
(Charles Pellegrini)

VETERANS ADMINISTRATION OFFICE:
810 Vermont Avenue NW,
Washington,
DC204020
U.S.A.

8TH AIR FORCE HISTORICAL SOCIETY:
P.O. Box 3556,
Hollywood,
FL33083,
U.S.A.

THE AMERICAN EMBASSY:
24, Grosvenor Square,
London, W1A 2LQ,
U.K.